SAILINGS

BRIGHTON

Palace Pier and West Pier

"GLEN GOWER, "WAVERLEY"

es see bottom of bill

BRIGHTON and SHANKLIN, SANDOWN or RYDE

st book the day before)   See special leaflets

t Pier 11.10 a.m.   Back 12.50 p.m.

er 2.30 p.m.; West Pier 2.40 p.m.
ave Ventnor 7.0 p.m.   Back 10.10 p.m.   **Fares: Single 4/-; Return 4/6**

r 2.30 p.m.; West Pier 2.40 p.m.
.0 p.m.; West Pier 3.10 p.m.   Back 5.20 p.m.

m.; Palace Pier 6.50 p.m.   Back 9.20 p.m.

est Pier 11.20 a.m.   Back 12.50 p.m.

.   Leave Eastbourne 4.20 or 8.40 p.m.   Back 5.40 or 10.0 p.m.
Fares: Returning at 4.20 p.m., **2/6**; at 8.40 p.m., **3/-**

.30 p.m.; Palace Pier 6.40 p.m.
Leave Eastbourne 8.40 p.m.   Back 10.0 p.m.   **Fare 2/-, Single or Return**

WHITE FUNNEL MAGIC

NIGEL COOMBES

TWELVEHEADS PRESS

TRURO • 1995

CONTENTS

TWELVEHEADS PRESS

First published 1995 by Twelveheads Press,
Chy Mengleth, Twelveheads, Truro, Cornwall TR4 8SN.
ISBN 0 906294 34 7
British Library Cataloguing-in-Publication Data.
A catalogue record for this book is available from the British Library.

Printed by The Amadeus Press Ltd., Huddersfield, Yorks.

INTRODUCTION
THE FAMOUS BLUE PENNANT

The speculative appearance of a small, Scottish paddle steamer, called the *Waverley*, in the River Avon in the summer of 1887 caused a flurry of interest in Bristol shipping circles. It was hardly a momentous occasion, even if the maiden trip was accompanied by the usual press razzmatazz. There were, however, to be remarkable consequences for the social life of the Bristol Channel.

Two brothers, Peter and Alec Campbell, had chartered their steamer *Waverley* to a Bristol syndicate which sought to chance its luck in the emerging local excursion business. What followed was a magical story of success and enterprise whose legacy, over a hundred years later, still nurtures the instinct to make today's channel cruising a way of life for many people.

The return of the Campbell brothers in 1888, using Bristol as their centre, accelerated a rationalisation of the steamer network. With a planned building programme of fast, attractive paddle steamers, they asserted a relentless hold over the Bristol Channel pleasure business. Pockett's Swansea–Ilfracombe link, alone, remained outside their

Much care was lavished on the carving of the paddle-boxes. Originally named the *Barry*, this ship joined Campbells in December 1911, retaining that name until March 1925 when she became the second *Waverley*. She still displays the magnificent crest of the Barry Railway Company, 'a stag at gaze, and a dragon passant'. Though both beasts are gilt here, the dragon was red in her Barry days and the scroll (now Campbell blue) green, with the gilt legend BARRY RAILWAY CO.
Edwin Keen

sphere of influence until after the First World War, although brief (and often cut-throat) competition was waged elsewhere at various times.

The atmosphere of those exciting early days helps to put the Campbells' achievement into perspective but the main thrust of this book is to capture the flavour of Bristol Channel cruising down the years. The company's extended arm on the South Coast is also covered: after all, it was an achievement by Bristol ships, staffed predominantly by Bristol crews. I feel that the cross–channel trips, for example, have never been properly recognised in the context of the Bristol story.

Passengers have always felt a strong affinity with, and affection for, the ships of the White Funnel fleet. It is a continuing strand which runs through these pages, paralleled by the camaraderie of staff, officers and crews whose photographs appear here, along with the steamers in which they served.

The excursion trade was a tough and demanding career to

follow but personnel took a great pride in their company. I hope that I have successfully broken new ground by looking at more than just the ships themselves. It has certainly been a delight to breathe a contemporary relevance into photographs of people, places and special occasions from the very earliest of years right up to the present.

Campbells were not only an institution but also a household name throughout South Wales and the west country. Down both sides of the Bristol Channel you merely had to say that you were 'going on Campbells' for your meaning to be immediately clear. If you remarked that you had 'been on *the* Campbells', the image of a paddle steamer with white funnels sprang to mind. Both were curious linguistic subtleties of their age. I do not believe any other company achieved quite such distinction.

Their tradition of Bristol Channel cruising came to a sad end in 1980 with the withdrawal of the last ship to fly the famous blue pennant with white chevron and ball, the motor passenger cruiser *Balmoral*. Happily, the resilience of that tradition found an established company prepared to carry it

The *Devonia* carried the coat of arms of the City of Exeter, Devon, on her paddle-boxes–the same three castles, incidentally, found on Exeter silverware. Photographed 13 May 1937 alongside Hotwells Road, Bristol with Bryan Bros. garage behind. Campbell paddlers were given fan vents so this design of hooped louvres betrays *Devonia*'s original lineage as a Red Funnel, Barry & Bristol Channel Steamship Company steamer. The castle motifs were carried from 1920 onwards.

Bristol Museum

on: now, another paddle steamer *Waverley*–with the same name as Campbells' original ship–and the restored *Balmoral*, still furrow the Bristol Channel's waters for a new generation's pleasure. In the wake of their forebears these two ships also ply the old routes on the South Coast.

Without taking anything away from my passionate support for the *Waverley* and the *Balmoral*, I am convinced that their success owes much to the White Funnel magic which went before.

The final chapter of this book is the most important one: in text and photograph the White Funnel inheritance is brought up to the present with 'The *Waverley* Years'. Bristol Channel cruising history is still in the making. Long may it continue...

Pictures of steamers at Burnham-on-Sea are quite scarce. The principal reason for ships to call there was to maintain a connection between Cardiff and Burnham, latterly in conjunction with the railway line opened on 10 September 1863 through to Poole and then on to Bournemouth.

One of the paddlers on this route was *The Lady Mary* (179 tons) built at Port Glasgow by Blackwood and Gordon in 1868. After service between Ardrossan and Arran, she was bought by John Boyle (Bute Trustees), of Cardiff, in 1874 and transferred to William T. Lewis in 1887 (for the newly formed Bute Docks Company).

Grahame Farr notes that the original railway connection from Burnham Pier to Highbridge Wharf had been opened on 3 May 1858, but this picture of *The Lady Mary* was probably taken in 1882-3 when, with the *Wye*. she maintained the Welsh connection. She travelled widely in the Bristol Channel and was scrapped in 1890.

Grahame Farr collection

Severn House – Royal Parade – Y° Miss Broad –

Burnham

H. G. Mounter, 64 Alfred St., Burnham.   H. M. Cooper, Photographer, Burnham.

Despite the railhead down to the slipway and the optimism of the Barry Railway Company on the other side of the channel, Burnham never really caught on as a route to the South Coast. The lack of water was probably the final arbiter as can be seen in this picture. The steamer is the *Cambria* and a 1904 postmark on the reverse of this postcard gives some idea of the date.

Edwin Hunt of Towcester had often chartered local paddle steamers for special excursions. He went one better than that when he bought and operated the steamer *Heather Bell* out of Bristol in the 1901 and 1902 seasons. The *Heather Bell* (271 grt) was already an elderly ship, having been built in 1871 by Blackwood and Gordon at Port Glasgow for service between Ardrossan and Arran. Subsequently in five years on the South Coast she had two different owners and Edwin Hunt, in fact, acquired her from a scrap merchant. After two indifferent years on the Bristol Channel, she went for good this time to Dutch breakers.

Edwin Hunt's *Heather Bell* was in the Bristol Channel so briefly that any photograph of her is worth recording. She is seen here at the railway slip at Burnham, with her light grey hull, in 1901.

Grahame Farr collection

An excellent view of Pockett's *Mavis* (474 grt), built in 1888 for the General Steam Navigation Company's Thames services, taken in Cumberland Basin, Bristol. The great bonded warehouse is seen behind. Pockett's Bristol Channel Steam Packet Co. Ltd. operated between Swansea and Ilfracombe and also owned the excursion paddler *Brighton*. Though not directly competing with Campbells their ships also called at Clovelly.

Howard H. Davies

This Batten study of the *Mavis*, taken at Ilfracombe on 8 June 1911 is a rare close-up of the foredeck and the bridge lay-out. Pockett had bought her in August 1910 but she ceased sailings at the end of the 1913 season.

Lin Bryant collection

THE GREAT POLL TAX AFFAIR

'Ugly Scenes at Hotwells Pontoon', 'Official Assaulted', 'Poll Tax Defied'; surely, these are not headlines associated with the relaxing pleasures of a paddle steamer excursion down the River Avon?

Surprisingly such incidents did, indeed, occur at Hotwells during the mid-1890s when a local *cause celebre* excited passions to fever pitch. It was all the Bristol Town Council's fault.

Casting a covetous eye at the large daily queues at the landing stage, the Docks Committee hatched a cunning plan; it was claimed that crowds awaiting the steamers prevented the ropemen from securing the steamers to the bollards. Railings, the Committee felt, were the obvious answer to restrain the passengers and they were duly installed. Then, at a full Council meeting on 16 March 1894 the blow fell; a resolution to impose tolls on all steamer passengers was passed by 25 votes to 15.

What became known as 'The Poll Tax' was highly unpopular and resentment grew throughout the season. A storm in a tea-cup, just so much froth in the paddle-box, the Council were convinced, it would all blow over... How wrong they were! There was a heated gathering at that hot-bed of Campbell loyalty, the Royal Hotel on College Green, and the outcome on 24 May 1895 was the formation of the Marine Excursionists' Protection Association.

The fight was on! A deputation met the Docks Committee and, on the following day, 11 June, a friend at court, Cllr. M. Levy, raised the poll tax question at a full Council. Public meetings were quickly called by political, ratepayers and trades organisations which all passed

‘ Ugly Scenes at Hotwells Pontoon ’

resolutions in favour of the excursionists' aim of abolishing the tolls.

The temperature of debate rose dramatically when the Association made an unexpected move. Sensing the Council's obstinacy it put up Cdr. George Cawley, R.N.R., to fight the Clifton ward in the November elections on an anti-Poll Tax ticket. Much to the excursionists' delight Cawley came top of the poll and was able to engage the enemy at closer quarters.

The whole bizarre affair came to a head in June 1896. An intending passenger, Mr. Simmons, took police proceedings for assault against Mr. Gray, the toll collector and, by way of riposte, the Docks Committee instituted

The cover for the menu of the Marine Excursionists' banquet on 9 February 1898 was composed by the celebrated Bristol artist F. G. Lewin, whose sketches and postcards are currently held in high regard by local collectors. Within the cover, the toast list ('interspersed with music') appeared unfettered by any constraints of time... or, indeed, capacity.
Ken Jenkins

So this was what all the fuss was about! The low-slung chains at Hotwells Pontoon allow the ropemen to work unhindered, for passengers to congregate behind them unmolested (and without charge...). The absence of a lifeboat forward of the *Britannia*'s paddle-box makes this a pre-1913 photograph.

Lionel Vaughan collection

Court action against excursionists on two occasions for not paying their tolls. There was a certain satisfaction that the toll collector in the first case was fined ten shillings, with five shillings costs.

The case for the excursionists had always been that the council interfered with traditional rights and privileges established by Ancient Charter. By the time a firm of solicitors had begun their study of old documents, the Council saw which way the wind was blowing and, amidst great jubilation, the repugnant Poll Tax was withdrawn on 14 July 1896.

There was complete satisfaction when Arthur Levy-Langfield – better known as the compiler of the delightful White Funnel Handbooks – was also elected in November 1896 to steer measures through the Council to substitute posts and chains for the hated railings. It was a total victory for the Association; Bristol day-trippers had won the day!

Far from dissolution, the Bristol Marine Excursionists' Protection Association extended their camaraderie to jolly banquets at the Royal Hotel–there was one in 1898–and also to supporting dissident Welsh trippers who were having similar Poll Tax problems with the Bute Estate in Cardiff. After the fuss at Bristol the Bute authorities wisely dropped the idea.

Competing steamers are berthed at Hotwells, Bristol, in this early picture from 1894. The *Westward Ho* – in her first season – is ahead (for P&A Campbell) and the *Lorna Doone* is astern (for Edwards, Robertson & Company). In the foreground is the Rownham ferry.

George Owen collection

THE *LORNA DOONE*

The *Lorna Doone* (405 grt) built in 1891 was an Edwards, Robertson & Company steamer. Her builders were Napier, Shanks and Bell, Glasgow. There was intense competition between her Cardiff owners and Campbells on the flagship Bristol–Ilfracombe run, but in October 1895 she passed to John Gunn of Cardiff and thence to the Southampton, Isle of Wight and South of England Royal Mail Steam Packet Co. Ltd. in 1898.

Certainly the *Lorna Doone* was a fine steamer, fast and well appointed; here was a match for Campbell's *Ravenswood* (1891), but not for the combined might of the *Westward Ho* (1894), the *Cambria* (1895) and the *Britannia* (1896), the three magnificent

There was music on board; the *Lorna Doone*'s band plays.
Ilfracombe Museum

White Funnel paddlers added in successive years.

The year before the Campbell trio began to match up to the opposition, 1893, was an interesting one. It was on the 5 June, that year, when the *Ravenswood* and the *Lorna Doone* collided, without injury to passengers, in a race for Weston Pier. For the *Lorna Doone* the 1893 season had opened on Wednesday, 29 March and an account in that week's Clevedon Mercury reflected the prose of more than just a local correspondent. Perhaps a well placed complimentary ticket evoked the right response! Savour for yourself the heady tones of Victorian commercial hyperbole;

That popular and fast pleasure steamer, the *Lorna Doone*, had her opening trip on

The *Lorna Doone* was a contemporary of the *Ravenswood*. She passed to John Gunn of Cardiff in 1895 and thence to the Southampton, Isle of Wight & South of England Royal Mail Steam Packet Co. Ltd., in 1898, whom she served until broken up in 1948. It was a long and honourable career but Campbell's *Ravenswood* still managed to outlive her by seven years. *The late Ernest Dumbleton*

Wednesday, the weather being charming. The approach to Cumberland Basin showed how interesting the occasion was to sightseers, there being a very large crowd present to watch the departure of the graceful vessel. Many were the comments of praise as she left the berth and, under the skilful care of Captain Hucker, proceeded at a capital pace down stream.

The attendance of passengers was numerous, and a band of musicians on board played some capital selections of music, the favourite airs from the pantomime forming an important part of the programme.

The voyage down the river was rendered interesting by the fact that there was more than the usual amount of shipping, but the experienced captain did not find it necessary to reduce speed, and soon the *Lorna Doone* was in the open, and breasting the waves in the direction of Clevedon.

On passing the *Formidable* training ship, the boys saluted the steamer with ringing cheers, which were answered by some of the younger generation on board. The course was taken past Portishead to the lightship and as the coast was closely 'hugged' some capital views were obtained, the green fields with the background of trees forming a pretty landscape.

The return journey was made in excellent time and the trip up the river was very enjoyable, the high tide covering the ugly mud banks, which offer such obstacles to navigation, and spoil the beauty of the scenery.

Below left: A lady passenger enjoys the view. Notice the foot-rest; light chalk marks the positioning of the furniture.

Below right: A master and his ship. Capt. Nat Hucker on the bridge of the *Lorna Doone* at Tenby.   *Ilfracombe Museum*

The decks of the *Lorna Doone* are very busy as she pulls out from Ilfracombe Pier, sometime in the 1892 season.   *Ilfracombe Museum*

With hindsight it seems inconceivable that such a well appointed steamer as the *Lorna Doone* should have been run off the Bristol Channel in a mere seven years. That, however, is what Campbell paddle power irresistibly managed to achieve. Neither should we forget that for one of those years, 1896, from early July to the end of September, the *Lorna Doone* was chartered by John Gunn to the Brighton, Worthing and South Coast Steamboat Company.

In a series of quite remarkable photographs, discovered recently in Ilfracombe Museum, life on board the *Lorna Doone* was vividly depicted. I am grateful to the Curator, Mrs. J. Slocombe, for permission to reproduce them.

FIGHTING WITH DRAGONS
THE RED FUNNEL THREAT

The compelling reason for Campbell's withdrawal from the Clyde in the 1880s had been the denial of access for their steamers at the growing number of railway piers. Their move to the Bristol Channel in 1888, having tested the water with the *Waverley* in the previous season, was a direct consequence of the railway steamers' monopoly of the Clyde.

It looked as if history was about to be repeated when, in 1905, the Barry Railway Company introduced their splendid pair of two-funnelled paddlers, the *Gwalia* and the *Devonia* which, with the older *Westonia*, and the *Barry* in 1907, seemed set to present a similar threat.

The railway company's base at Barry gave a fiercely competitive service to Weston; with Cardiff close by there was a gifted opportunity to embark the cream of Weston pier's down-channel traffic to Ilfracombe.

Campbells responded with a successfully fought case through the courts – even though the judgement was contested with some subterfuge over three years – by which the Barry Railway Company were obliged to start and finish their excursions at their home port, thus abiding by the original terms of their charter.

The restrictions were too severe on what had become popularly known as the Red Funnel Line and, in 1910, the *Devonia*, the *Westonia* and the *Barry* were sold to another South Wales company. Two years later the trio were run by Campbells; not quite a total triumph...for it was to be a further ten years before the *Gwalia* passed into White Funnel colours, as the *Lady Moyra*.

An unusual photo of the *Devonia*, dating from her Red Funnel days circa 1906. She is pictured arriving at the entrance to the second, up-river lock at Cumberland Basin, Bristol. The recesses for the gates can still be seen in the wall to-day. *Grahame Farr collection*

It is a delight to view the spacious and tastefully furnished rooms below. The comfortable saloon of the *Gwalia* is particularly pleasing with its carpeting and plush upholstery. There is a writing desk in the centre, barometer on the left panel and chronometer on the right; note, too, the half curtains to let in the light but to keep out the sun.   *Scottish Record Office*

Inscribed BARRY STEAMSHIPS 1905, the gilded relief of the company's coat of arms is magnificently outlined on the *Gwalia*'s paddle-box. The circular design of the vents helps to distinguish the Red Funnel paddlers from Campbell's.

Scottish Record Office

Main photograph: The *Gwalia* ran two preliminary Clyde trials on 16 and 20 March 1905, on one of which occasions this striking photograph was almost certainly taken. A subsequent official trial shot shows her with house-flag and name pennant. Working at full speed would cause the funnels to discolour with heat so, here, the gantlines are still in place for repainting. Both the *Gwalia* and the *Devonia* were built by John Brown & Company, Clydebank.

Scottish Record Office

It is often a photographer's nightmare to find a suitable angle on a set of engines in a paddle-steamer. This fascinating shot, before installation and taken at John Brown's engineering shop, is said to feature the compound set destined for the *Devonia* (1905).

Scottish Record Office

A special photograph, this shows the Barry and Bristol Channel Steamship Company's *Gwalia* in her pristine, original colours at the start of her first season between April and mid-May, 1905. The black-tipped buff funnels thereafter changed to red with deeper black tops. A later postcard of this magnificent Cardiff Pierhead shot was ruined by shaking and a double image resulted!

The late Dr. Richards

A striking view of the arrival of the *Gwalia* (also indicated on the name-board of the Red Funnel booking office). She must be fairly close to her complement judging by her crowded decks; a good day for the company and for the Ilfracombe shop-keepers!

All available steamers were at Cardiff on 13 July 1907 for the opening of the Queen Alexandra Dock by King Edward VII. It was a public holiday in Cardiff and it was estimated that 100,000 attended the opening ceremony. Amidst the jumble of masts and bunting can be seen the two funnels (with the bridge behind the funnels) of the *Westonia*, next *The Marchioness* and on the right either *Devonia* or *Gwalia*. The latticed railway-style signals controlled shipping movements at the pontoons.

The *Westonia* passed out of the Barry Railway Company's hands (1905-9) to Bristol Channel Passenger Boats Ltd., Cardiff for the two seasons following. This photograph from slightly ahead of the beam, taken by Wehrley of Penarth (probably in 1910), shows the *Westonia* to her best advantage.

Photographs taken on board the *Westonia* are fairly rare. The handbill attached to the deck-house confirms that this is a Red Funnel paddler, taken between 1905 and 1910. It seems to be a photo of the catering staff – the uniforms are those of stewards – and the man in the peaked cap is most likely the deck-chair attendant. For me the most appealing feature is the young chocolate boy sitting cheerfully cross-legged in the front of the group. He plied the decks with his tray, wearing a very smart cap with its Cadbury's hat-band.

It is unusual to find the three Barry Railway Company paddlers together. Local photographer Heber Shirvington took the trio at Barry pontoon in the 1908–9 period. The *Barry* is on the outside, the *Devonia* and the *Gwalia* nearer the pontoon; it is hard to tell the sisters apart from astern.   *George Owen*

The officers and crew of Campbell's original *Waverley* feature in this fine, formal group photograph taken on board at Newport Pontoon in 1896. Capt. Allan Livingstone (fingers linked) is seated in the centre; sitting on his left is Joe Ashford, the Mate. Tasteful airs were offered by the banjo player (left) and guitarist (right). The notice is quite explicit; NO PASSENGERS ALLOWED ON THE PADDLE-BOXES. PASSENGERS ARE REQUESTED NOT TO STRIKE MATCHES ON THE PAINTWORK.

George Owen collection

A CAPTAIN AND HIS SHIP
JOE ASHFORD AND THE *WAVERLEY*

An invaluable early member of the Campbell team was Capt. Joe Ashford. One of twelve children, he was born in 1866 at Nore Farm, Portishead. Joe's father, also Joseph, was in the 300-year-old family tradition of farmer/fisherman so, among the sons, it was natural that Joe and Clarence (in tugs) should go to sea while Jim took on the farm.

The young Joe, educated at St Barnabas School, Portishead, was apprenticed to Sharpness Pilots and became fully qualified after deep-sea service. Since Campbells regularly ran cruises up the Wye and Severn, Capt. Ashford's outstanding knowledge of the area was a great asset. He went full time with the company at the turn of the century sometimes as Mate and then as Captain of the first *Waverley*, finally retiring from the *Westward Ho* in 1934/35.

Ashore Jim's son, 'Young' Jim continued to farm and to tend Black Nore lighthouse, though the fishing - for sprats - ceased in 1932. In all, the Ashfords served Trinity House for 84 years, well after Nore Farm was sold in 1953. In foggy weather, perhaps as a result of the *Albion*'s stranding at Black Nore in 1907, the family would always blow a whistle to warn the paddlers where they were.

Affectionately, 'Young' Jim Ashford spoke of those years between the world wars; 'We watched out for the Campbells - especially if it was Uncle Joe. I learned to recognise them all by sight, but you could hear the *Britannia* a mile away. She had a squeak in her paddle-box. They never managed to cure it!'

Another happy diversion helps to illustrate the strong bonds which tied the pleasure-steamer families together. As the darker autumn evenings drew in, the sound of paddle-floats came up sharply on the wind. 'We had no electric light at Nore Farm in those days,' Jim explained. 'So, when we heard the beat of paddles, we'd lift the oil lamps off the table, step outside the door and wave them. We'd always get the answer back. They'd blow, for us, as they went past.'

This splendid Victorian portrait of Capt. Joe Ashford, later to be master of the *Waverley*, was taken in the studio of Atkins & Lockyear at Newport.
Jim Ashford

Atkins & Lockyear   NEWPORT MON.

S.S. BONNIE DOON.

The *Bonnie Doon* was acquired by P. & A.
Campbell in March 1899; here she is pictured
in the Usk, just after leaving Newport. Her thin
funnel places the date as pre-1907.

Newport Bridge is in the background for this picture of the *Scotia's* crew during her service with Campbells (1899–1903). Seated at the top of the steps are, left to right, Fred Nunn (Mate), Capt. Hector McFadyen, Bob Wilson (Ch. Engineer).

George Owen collection

Photographs from below decks are, not surprisingly, rare from the early days; it must have been quite a performance to set up the equipment and arrange the lighting. It is interesting, therefore to see the dining saloon of the *Scotia*. Edwards, Robertson & Co. ran her on the Bristol Channel from 1893 to 1895 and John Gunn had her from 1895 to 1899. The *Scotia* passed to Campbells in 1899 and remained in their service until 1903. The saloon seems spacious with typical turn-of-the-century furnishings and unlikely to have altered much during her various ownerships.

George Owen collection

RISE AND FALL: THE PIER AT WOODY BAY

There has always been an air of mystery about the pier at Woody Bay, partly because the structure was so short-lived and partly as a result of the scandal surrounding the tiny resort's developer at the time.

Pictures of the pier are rare; the call of the *Cambria*, reproduced in my book: *Passenger Steamers of the Bristol Channel*, evoked much interest but I expected little else to follow. Hence my huge delight in the discovery of a photographic sequence – located through the kindness of Mrs. Harriet Bridle – of the rise and fall of Woody Bay Pier taken by the late Reverend Reginald Walter Oldham.

One can only speculate on the difficulties encountered in hauling the massive timber baulks down the steep combe and competing with the tides to put them in place. Certainly, once completed, the pier with its cross-braced trestles evoked the spirit of the pioneers and would not have looked out of place across a remote gulch in the Wild West.

31 July 1896 – Two workmen pose beside the steam winch, wired for hauling up the heavy weight of the pile driver.

31 July 1896 – The construction team pose with the diver.

20 February 1896. – A start has been made.

13 June 1896 – The trestles are well advanced and some of the braces in place.

15 April 1897 – The pier is now complete, while 'the first boat that didn't call' passes down the coast.

Spring 1899 – The first great storm removed the shoreward trestles but the walkway has been repaired.

Woody Bay Pier was a brief and eccentric part of the Bristol Channel jig-saw. Campbell's steamers called occasionally and Pockett's *Brighton* a mere three times. Some passengers would stay at the hotel but you could, theoretically, make the steep ascent to Woody Bay station and holiday in Lynton or find business in Barnstaple; a pretty way to go…

I am indebted to Flt. Lieut. John Oldham, grandson of the photographer, for his permission to reproduce these fascinating pictures. Mrs. Bridle's delightful book *Woody Bay* tells the story of this unusual place.

30 December 1900 – A second hurricane the previous day has caused an irreparable breach.

11 June 1902 – The damage wrought by the elements is plain to see. Just a year later there was nothing left.

Three steamers at Ilfracombe sometime
between 1907 and 1909; the *Cambria*, the
Devonia (red funnels) and the *Westward Ho*
outside. The *Devonia*'s white ribbon at the
waterline confirms the date.

Few stories of heroic endeavour have gripped the public's imagination more completely than the polar exploits of Capt. Robert Falcon Scott, R.N. The expedition, which was to culminate in Scott's epic trip to the South Pole, left Cardiff on 15 June 1910 on board the ex-whaler *Terra Nova*. Campbell's *Ravenswood*, packed with well-wishers and bedecked with flags, was there to bid the *Terra Nova* bon voyage.

George Owen collection

A picture, taken at Bristol, of the *Princess May* in March 1902. She had been bought the previous month by the Campbell brothers, on their own account, from the liquidators of the Brighton, Worthing and South Coast Steam Boat Company. The *Princess May* went south at the end of June 1902 for the Spithead Review and was then sold. Here, she is in the colours of her previous owner, having arrived from Shoreham.

George Owen collection

Campbells prided themselves on their catering department. Much prominence is given in the early channel guides to dining facilities as an essential part of any trip. Indeed, revenue from the dining saloon, bars and sales of chocolate – for all of which the Chief Steward was responsible – made the catering staff an integral part of each ship's company.

In this dignified study of the catering crew (most probably on the *Britannia* but possibly the *Cambria*) taken in Bristol about 1900, the Chief Steward, Frank Tyrrell, stands on the left. He has evidently told young William Hewlett, next to him, to look smart, stand up straight and put his shoulders back! Frank's son, Albert Tyrrell, stands shirt-sleeved at the other end of the row.

There was to be a magical postscript. When I showed the photograph to Dorothy Partington in Bristol recently, almost a hundred years after the picture was taken, she immediately identified her grandfather and her father, Albert, as a young man. She had never seen it before. It was, for me, a wonderful moment of poignancy and pleasure.

10 CLOVELLY. — *Passengers Embarking.* — LL.

Landings at Clovelly are always full of human interest as this splendidly animated L. Levy view shows. Small boats, sculled from the stern by a single oar, are taking passengers out to the *Lady Ismay* probably in 1912 or 1913. Lifeboats were added, forward, in 1914.

G. E. Langmuir

A very useful addition to Campbell's fleet in 1911, the *Lady Ismay* (495 grt) was the first of three similar pre-war paddlers built by the Ailsa Shipbuilding Company, Troon. Her passenger capacity of 1,020 on the Weston ferry service came in handy. *Lady Ismay*'s career was a short one; called up for war service in December, 1914, as a minesweeper she was mined and sunk on 21 December 1915, off the Longsand Light Vessel.

As a study in contemporary social poise and tastes in fashion I found this photograph irresistible. A cruise before the First World War was a Sunday best occasion; waistcoats were almost universally worn by the men for whom headgear embraced the bowler, trilby, boater and flat cap. The ladies' hats are magnificent and, no doubt, firmly anchored! Notice, too, how many of the men are smoking pipes. In the short time available, Batten, the Ilfracombe photographer, has overcome the confines of space to contrive as perfect a group as he could manage; heads are in gaps or cunningly outlined against darker clothing. The stars at the centre of this little stage, on the *Lady Ismay*'s foredeck on 24 July 1912, are the formidable matron in the black dress and the supremely nonchalant young man leaning against the rail. The picture is a small tribute to the artistry and professionalism of the sea-side photographer. *Lin Bryant*

OFFICIAL POSTCARDS 1912–14

P. & A. Campbell commissioned a magnificent set of official postcards for the 1912-14 seasons. How ironic that the cards had such a short run! Since the war intervened these views are the rarest which collectors are likely to discover. Some of the photographs were used to illustrate the 1914 Bristol Channel Guide so they must have been shot in the previous seasons. A homely feature of the 1914 Guide – subsequently discontinued – was the list of Captains which I have included here.

The photo of the *Waverley*, Campbell's first ship of that name (and not to be confused with the renamed *Barry* in

1912–14 postcard set and their Captains in the 1914 season		
Albion.	Eastbourne.	Capt. J. Trenance.
Barry.	Penarth.	Capt. J. H. Denman.
Brighton Queen.	Eastbourne.(both)	Capt. H. McFadyen.
Glen Avon.	Penarth.	Capt. J. N. Webber.
Ravenswood.	Eastbourne.	Capt. D. James.
Waverley.	Eastbourne.	Capt. J. Knight.
Westward Ho.	Penarth.	Capt. J. Ashford.
Not pictured.		
Britannia.	Capt. D. Taylor.	
Cambria.	Capt. A. Livingstone.	
Glen Rosa.	Capt. R. J. Webber.	
Lady Ismay.	Capt. H. Chidgey.	
Devonia.	Capt. D. Ryan.	
Glen Usk.		

the inter-war years) bears the name of the Eastbourne photographer W. A. Pelly, also the local Agent. It is certain that Pelly took the other South Coast studies but whether he also took the Bristol Channel trio is debatable; perhaps a Penarth photographer, Andrew Lindstrom, George Wehrley or R. Tanner, was responsible, but, that said, the cards carry similar front printing and identical backs.

The clarity and sharpness of the cards is exciting. The urgency of the *Albion* and the *Ravenswood* profiles is most

P. & A. CAMPBELL'S LTD.,   PLEASURE STEAMER 'ALBION'.   COPYRIGHT.

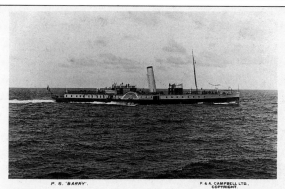

P. S. 'BARRY'.   P. & A. CAMPBELL LTD., COPYRIGHT.

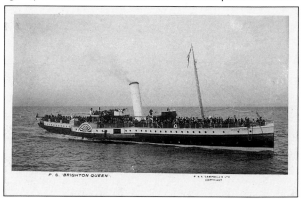

P. S. 'BRIGHTON QUEEN'.   P. & A. CAMPBELL'S LTD COPYRIGHT.

satisfying; the well judged silhouettes of the *Glen Avon* and *Westward Ho* make the best of the afternoon light, while the funnel's reflection in the latter study - and the stark outline of the dark figure on the paddle-box - balanced by smoke above and a gently curving wave on the foreshore create an outstanding effect of tranquillity and graceful power. The *Brighton Queen*, well passengered, Captain bent over the bridge telegraph, captures an imminent pier call to perfection.

W. A. Pelly was Campbell's Agent at Eastbourne from 1905 to 1939. He was not, incidentally, a professional photographer but a gifted amateur.

P. S. 'RAVENSWOOD'

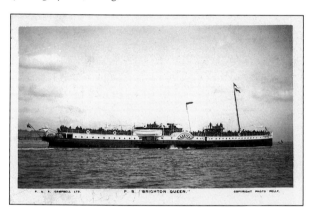

P. S. "BRIGHTON QUEEN."

P.S. "WAVERLEY."

P. S. "GLEN AVON".

P. S. 'WESTWARD HO'

This splendid aerial photograph of the *Glen Avon* at Newport gives an idea of the layout of the pontoon; an uncomplicated arrangement of two huts, three bench seats and a door in the wall at the rear of Davies Bros., builders' merchants.

Note the schooner delivering a cargo of building material. Davies Bros. continues in business today, as Deebees.

The pontoon was last used in 1956 and towed away in 1957. The Waverley and the Balmoral now use Blaina Wharf, downstream on the other side of the River Usk.

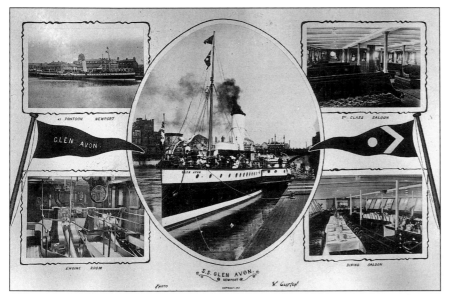

One of the delights of collecting old postcards is the picture on the front; this composite viewcard of the *Glen Avon* by W. Clifton of Newport gives glimpses of the engine room and saloons. The centre feature was already in use as a card in its own right and it serves to show the uses for which a photographer would employ his material. The other delight is to use the postmark for various purposes of dating; this card was posted in Weston at 4.45 p.m. on 5 August 1913. Bert Marfleet, the writer, confirms that, 'this is a photo of the boat we came by' to his parents at 57 Deacon Street, Swindon. Such intimate pieces of social history should, by rights, rest with the family concerned but it is far better that they should be rescued than irretrievably lost.

PASSENGER BOATS, BARRY PIER

Passengers, some of the men in boaters, make their way up the *Waverley*'s gangway at Barry; some of them are for the *Westward Ho* which they board by the simple expedient of a gangway slung between the two paddle-boxes. The Barry lifeboat slip is partly hidden by the *Westward Ho*'s funnel. The picture just pre-dates the First World War. George Owen remarks that this shot must be from the 1913 season; the *Westward Ho* has lifeboats on the fore sponsons but the *Waverley* (inside) has yet to add the single extra lifeboat on the fore sponson for the 1914 season.

TYRRELL FAMILY

The loyalty of whole families was a notable feature of the White Funnel Fleet's personnel. Two Campbell sons, Bob and Alec, joined the company, and there were the Birminghams and the Taylors.

For one family, however - the Tyrrells - service in the fleet assumed an almost dynastic dimension. Frank Tyrrell rose to become a Chief Steward in Campbell's earliest days, the first member of the family in a tradition which spanned three generations. His son Bert, whose wife Emily joined the team, also became a Chief Steward and Catering Superintendent on the South Coast between the wars. There was Harry Tyrrell and his wife Elsie, and Ada Tyrrell. Bert's son, Reg Tyrrell, and daughter Dorothy both followed in father's footsteps on the catering side.

Elsie Tyrrell was born in 1899 but clearly recalls the 'twenties and 'thirties and the excitement of working as a stewardess for a big shipping company; 'Fog was sometimes a problem on the cross-Channel trips and on board you had to put in a lot of hours but there were nice shops in Boulogne and a bazaar which we used to visit. One year, going round Land's End, a storm broke the porthole in the chef's galley and we had to put into Falmouth for two days.' After the Second World War, Elsie served in three Queens; the *Bristol Queen, Cardiff Queen* and, finally, *Queen of the Isles* – she was specially called out of retirement in 1968 for the last venture.

The unique flavour of those inter-war years was wonderfully brought to life by Dorothy Partington (née Tyrrell), now in her nineties. 'I started with Campbells in 1923. Mother (Emily) and Father (Bert) were on the *Bonnie Doon* before the First War and Mother was stewardess on the *Brighton Queen*. For three years, before the Second World War started we lived in Belle Vue Gardens, Brighton,

A cheerful group of officers and crew on the *Glen Gower*. Seated at each end are two unidentified seamen then, left to right, Spencer Solomon (Chief Engineer), Mrs. Bruford, Captain William Bruford, Elsie Tyrrell (Stewardess), Fred Smyth (Mate); Sid Partington (Purser) is behind Mrs. Bruford and Dorothy Partington (Stewardess) behind the Mate. Mr. Smyth was killed during the war and was a son of Arthur E. Smyth, Campbell's Swansea Agent.

The late Clifton Smith-Cox identified Ventnor as the unusual venue and 18 May 1935 as the date.
Clevedon Pier

Campbells' second *Waverley* (ex-*Barry*) was a regular 'South Coaster' in the inter-war years. The Tyrrell family are again represented, Ada seated left and Elsie on the right. A special lifebelt is inscribed with a company pennant and a Red Ensign; seated behind it is Capt. Weekes, who was later pier-master at Brighton's Palace Pier and whose son, Alan, is the well known broadcaster. Behind the galley-boy is Albert Jones, the Mate. The crews' peaked caps point to a photo from 1929 or subsequently.   *Elsie Tyrrell.*

during the season, though we had cabins on board.

'I was on the *Devonia* for twelve years and managed the tea-room.' Dorothy's future husband, Sid, transferred to the *Devonia* as Purser and Radio Officer; he was employed by Marconi but transferred to Campbell's. 'He asked me three times to go out for a meal, but I refused each time,' Dorothy remembered with amusement, 'and then he went home to Manchester! But we were engaged, and married at the end of the 1931 season.' Sid was also Chief Electrician for the company.

The *Devonia*'s base for the night, in company with the other Campbell paddlers, was Newhaven. When cruising was finished for the day the crews were able to enjoy an hour's social relaxation; 'We had to climb up an iron ladder on the 'railway' side, at Newhaven, to go ashore... that was fun... then I used to play the piano in The Ark! There was also one day off a week; often I'd go up to London with Mother on the train for our day off.'

Many details of a side of the *Devonia*'s life which passengers did not see were still vividly fixed in Dorothy Partington's memory; 'Catering for the crew was excellent. Always breakfast at 8, lunch at 12, tea at 5 and supper at 9.

You could always have a bowl of soup at any time, if you wanted it.' At night, after passengers had gone, curried lobster was a great favourite.

'During the trip, I served teas, cakes, chocolate, Bovril and coffee. The *Devonia* had gold settees, very smart. One passenger I remember used to come regularly, always on a Sunday; Lord Loftus – he was the son of the Marquis of Ely. As well as playing the piano, I had a ukulele; Lord Loftus would ask me if I would fetch it and then he'd play it himself. He always booked at eight for dinner...'

'We looked forward to going away to Brighton but it was nice to come home, to Bristol, at the end of the season.'

By mid-October, after the rigours of the cruising season, all the White Funnel paddle steamers, from near and far, were back in Bristol. Within a few hundred yards of each other, in Merchant's Dock, at Underfall Yard, ranged along Hotwells, as fine and graceful a fleet of excursion ships as you would ever see...

For the Tyrrells, however, it was time to re-establish their roots in their home city. The family restaurant (later to become Marco's) was at the top of St Nicholas' Steps, in the city, so there was plenty to do during the winter months.

Christmas and New Year was always the time for big family re-unions to which many company colleagues and friends were invited. Dororthy Partington recalled the occasions with tremendous pleasure; 'Home was in Ashley Hill. At Christmas we had quite a party; the Campbell sons, Alec and Bob, came; there were the Taylors, and the Cuthberts – they had The Priory, across the centre – and Nellie Campbell (who married Mr. Fry), and the McFadyens. We would have a bar set up and lots of food. Dad's suppliers were good to him; we had anything up to five turkeys sent round at Christmas. We lived off turkey until we could hardly face them. For the suppliers, perhaps the next season had something to do with it!'

This hard working, but settled, seasonal existence came to an abrupt end with the Second World War. Dorothy's

A Campbell's trio at Ilfracombe, between 1931 and 1933 when there was a Ghost Train on the pier! Fred Halse (Chief Engineer), Bert Tyrrell (Chief Steward), Charles Jenkins (Mate) with pipe are on the *Britannia*.   *Syd Gray*

sadness when news filtered through that the *Devonia* had been sunk at Dunkirk met an echo in many Bristol hearts.

TED COLE

From time to time former Campbell employees are welcomed aboard the *Balmoral* for a celebration cruise. In 1993, Ted Cole looked back seventy years to remember his early days as a chocolate boy in the *Glen Usk* at the beginning of the 'twenties. Like many connected with the steamers he lived in Clifton, in Albemarle Road, handy for early starts.

Ted's route up the company ladder was via deck-chair attendant to Ordinary Seaman, jersey smartly inscribed with the Campbell initials, seeing service on the *Britannia* and the *Ravenswood*. He vividly recalled his deck-chair days. Lynmouth was a very special occasion; 'We had some very nice people getting aboard from the small boat at Lynmouth. The man suffered from arthritis and I found them four seats. He put out his hand; there were three half-crowns. A lot of money in those days.'

The same party would often come out in the launch; 'I saw a lady with her arm raised, waving. I knew it was for me. I ran below for thick blankets and they had their chairs. Always three half-crowns. They were very grateful.'

Sundays were different. Wales was dry on the Sabbath. 'On a Sunday, the evening drinking cruise cost 2 shillings return from Newport and Cardiff to Minehead. That was in the 'twenties. We called it the 'boozers' trip'. After the day's sailings the crew went ashore at Cardiff; we saw the first talking picture at the Capitol in Queen Street.'

Seventy years later Ted Cole's greatest satisfaction is that his grandson, Nick Worthy (*see page 114*) became a member of the *Balmoral*'s deck crew. The family tradition in the Bristol Channel still lives on.

SYD GRAY

The exacting nature of a career in Campbell's catering department before the Second World War involved long hours and the maintenance of high standards. Syd Gray, who now lives in Banwell, Somerset, joined the company as a chocolate boy in 1933 and later became a Chief Steward; 'I started when I was 13 and I was paid two shillings and sixpence a day.' The competition for jobs in those days was intense. 'You had to be a skilled man; if you weren't, there were a hundred others to step into your shoes.'

August Bank Holiday Monday sailings were truly in the marathon class. In the early 'thirties, Syd recalls, the programme for one of those days meant reporting for duty down at the Hotwells stage at 4 a.m. with the steamer leaving Bristol for Ilfracombe (direct) within the hour. The steamer returned to Bristol, incorporating a morning cruise out of 'Combe. Then there would be a mid-day sailing from Bristol calling at Clevedon, Cardiff, Penarth, Barry, Lynmouth and Ilfracombe. This would be followed by an afternoon cruise from Ilfracombe, while the final sailing would be the long return haul up the Channel, making the stops in reverse order.

The return was sometimes to Avonmouth, where passengers caught a train from the passenger terminal, but the day was not yet over for the crew; there was clearing up to do. Bunkering and taking on water started at midnight, which took a couple of hours, before the steamer could finally call it a day. The paddles turned again at 5 a.m. for the short trip up to Bristol, arriving at 6; 'finished with engines', twenty-six hours almost non-stop, four hours sleep and a gruelling Bank Holiday schedule completed.

The programme did not always go to plan, however. Take Bank Holiday Monday, 4 August 1930, as an example. George Owen's invaluable notes recorded that

Right: A cheerfully informal portrait of Syd Gray in 1938 taken at Cardiff pontoon. He was dining-saloon cashier on board the *Britannia*. *Left:* Syd Gray (left) as Chief Steward of the *Empress Queen*.   *Syd Gray*

the *Britannia* arrived at Bristol at 3.45 a.m. from anchor, ready to take the scheduled 4.15 a.m. sailing to Minehead (6 shillings return) and Ilfracombe (7s 6d). While swinging in the river she struck the slip and damaged four floats. The *Glen Usk* was immediately drafted in to take the early excursion leaving at 4.35 a.m. – just twenty minutes late.

The *Britannia* went through to Tongue Head, the ends were cut off the floats and she left Bristol, light, at 1.25 p.m. for Cardiff, arriving at 3.25. After a run on the ferry service to Weston, she left Cardiff at 6.30 p.m. for Ilfracombe, where she arrived at 9.15 p.m. As her scheduled return was due to be away at 9.15 p.m. she was undoubtedly a few minutes late for departure to Minehead (11.00 p.m.) and thence back to Bristol direct (about 1.30 a.m. the following morning!)

As the slump of the early 'thirties eased, Syd progressed up the catering ladder; he became aware of the unusual

Some of the catering staff of the *Bristol Queen* - Syd Gray leaning against the rail – take a welcome breather at Ilfracombe. Peace without passengers!

Syd Gray

demands of the weekly routine and its changing clientele. 'On Mondays you had the fish-mongers and butchers; Tuesday and Wednesday attracted the publicans; Saturdays and Sundays were more for the general public.' Each trip from Bristol had its special atmosphere.

When Campbells resumed sailings after the war the world had changed. There was rationing, for one thing, and simple necessities such as toilet-paper and soap were in short supply and it was painfully evident to pre-war staff that the old standards could not be maintained. Syd's opinions were probably characteristic; 'After the war, things were different. All of us had come through the war; we were experienced. Campbells needed advice from their staff but didn't ask for it – particularly the catering staff and the engineers. We could have helped; for example, they issued new uniforms every year!'

There were other tangible signs which would add to White Funnel's difficulties. The heart was torn out of the city during the Bristol blitz and whole stretches of Hotwells were devastated by the bombing. The loss of patronage from the formerly thriving shops and businesses in Hotwells, within easy reach of the pontoon, was a serious blow, while the rehousing of residents in developments on the fringe of the city radically altered its demography. The

tram system – so convenient with its Hotwells terminus – had been destroyed and the Clifton Rocks Railway never ran after the war. Certainly, Campbell's had much to contend with.

To add to the company's woes, the base of the *Britannia*'s furnaces collapsed at Cardiff in July, 1946. It happened at 2 o'clock in the morning and Syd Gray vividly remembered the frightening episode, 'I was on board at the time. I closed the fire doors, told Capt. Brander and helped to get everyone out. All the varnish in the bar was blistered, and the heat was so intense that all the rims came away from the glasses racked above the bar.'

Syd transferred to the *Bristol Queen* for the rest of that season, saw service in the *Glen Gower* and the *Empress Queen* (1947-9), the *Bristol Queen* (1949-51) and finally two seasons on the *Cardiff Queen* (1952-3) before moving ashore to become Assistant Catering Manager at Woolworth's in Broadmead, Bristol.

The *Bristol Queen*'s dining saloon, looking aft. The woodwork was oak veneer with a mahogany trim.　　*Syd Gray*

The visit of the warship *HMS Lion* caused much local excitement when she anchored in Swansea Bay. The *Lady Moyra* picked up a huge crowd for the occasion on 11 September 1919 at Mumbles. William H. Tucker's Yellow Funnel Line were running the *Lady Moyra* in this first post-war season and subsequently until Campbells bought her in 1922. Every inch of the ship is packed from stem to stern and the port paddle-box is well under water.

George Owen collection

The *Lady Moyra* was sold by Tuckers to P & A Campbell in July 1922. She left Swansea under tow on 5 July and arrived at Campbell's wharf, Underfall Yard, the following day.

It was to be almost a year before she was prepared for service with her new owners. The *Lady Moyra* went into Stothert's dry dock, after attention to mast and funnels, on 5 June 1923. Here her mast was re-instated and she was also fitted with bilge keels, one of which can be seen. The mast and funnel stays are hanging loose but would have been tightened before leaving dry dock on 8 June; the photograph was probably taken between these two dates.

The *Lady Moyra* did a trial trip on 3 July, a charter trip from Briton Ferry to Ilfracombe on 14 July and then really got started four days later. I am indebted to George Owen for all these details.

Bristol Museum

Local promenaders have turned out in force to watch a busy *Lady Moyra* at Porthcawl sometime in the 1930 season.

George Owen collection

The relative merits of the two landing jetties at Weston's Birnbeck Pier are featured in this aerial photo reproduced from a half-tone block in an old guide book. The *Barry* is berthed at the southern arm which was completed in 1909 and dismantled in 1922. While under construction it was badly damaged by the heavy gale of 10 September 1903 which also swept away the old stage on the north side. There is also an extension of the pier 'railway', a wheeled conveyance from the pier gates for heavy luggage. Minehead's pier had one also.

George Owen collection

The *Glen Gower* arrives at Ilfracombe in 1922 or 1923. When Pockett's withdrew from the Swansea station there was an obvious opening for Campbells to operate in the West Wales area and between 1922, when she entered service, and 1934, when she went to the South Coast, *Glen Gower* was principally employed on the Swansea station for which she was built. There were calls at Porthcawl and Tenby and cruises to Mumbles and the Gower coast, but a regular run for *Glen Gower* was from Swansea and Mumbles across the Channel to Ilfracombe. She was a good-looking ship, compact and neatly proportioned, funnels tightly placed and with a pleasing sheer. For that reason her profile seemed quite different from all the others when seen wintering at Bristol with her consorts.

The late Ernest Dumbleton

The *Glen Gower* has just arrived at Ilfracombe from Swansea on what appears to have been a cold crossing judging by the heavy coats. The Mate, Jimmy Martin, is squaring up the gangways for disembarkation – always the Mate's job at this stage of the trip.

POSTCARDS

After the First World War, for a variety of reasons, the sale of picture postcards declined. There was, however, still a niche market for specialised local themes to place alongside the increasingly mass-produced views of the big publishers. The Avonmouth newsagents J. & C. McKenna published some magnificent shipping studies in the twenties, based on the docks at Avonmouth, featuring in particular the beautiful white ships of Elders & Fyffes, which ran to the West Indies in the passenger and banana trade.

Happily the photographer sometimes set up his camera on the Avon side of the docks; the result was a set of outstanding Campbell studies, limited in their location but of remarkable clarity and poise.

P.S. WESTWARD HO

P.S. GLEN USK   AVONMOUTH

P.S. WAVERLEY

Above: The *Glen Usk* makes a fine sight as she surges past Avonmouth into the Channel, out of sunshine and into the haze.

Above left: A packed *Westward Ho,* outward bound, passes Portbury Shipyard, whose workshops can be seen behind the funnel on the Somerset bank.

The *Ravenswood* approaches the mouth of the Avon. Portishead lies behind the paddler with Battery Point astern. We must excuse the photographer for his lapse in ship recognition.

Pleasure Steamer passing Shirehampton.

13377

Only a handful of postcards was issued showing pleasure steamers passing between Pill and Shirehampton. Occasionally the paddlers slowed for passengers to be embarked at Pill by rowing boat, but in this picture the *Westward Ho* shows no sign of calling. The Shirehampton Signal Station on the North bank of the Avon will have telephoned the steamer's progress up-river.

I have long been mystified by the appearance of furled sails on the Campbell paddlers. What were they for and were they ever used? George Owen unravels the mystery. 'All the steamers carried two sails – a Board of Trade requirement – the object being that if the engines broke down the ship could be sailed, but how this could be done with a shallow draught paddle steamer is another matter. I have seen the trysail used to reduce yawing when running before a heavy quartering sea, but never the jib. The requirement was rescinded in 1938 when the steamers ceased to carry them, but then the Board demanded weather cloths on the forward rails - another silly idea...'

The sails were kept in canvas covers. Here, the sails (jib forward and trysail abaft the mast) have been unfurled for drying. The steamer is the *Glen Usk*, anchored off Lundy in about 1929 or 1930 in a picture as fascinating as it is rare. *George Owen collection*

An important P&A Campbell event was the company dinner, held at a Bristol hotel after the end of the season: it was a good opportunity for shore, office and sea-going staff to meet in convivial surroundings. The company Chairman, W. G. Banks, is in the centre foreground; diagonally behind him to the wall notice on the left, are Fred Birmingham (Ilfracombe agent), Gerry Dascombe, Capt. Jack George, Capt. Henry Chidgey. On the right of the front row is Bill Churchyard (Company Secretary 1912-37). The picture seems to date from the inter-war years. *Syd Gray*

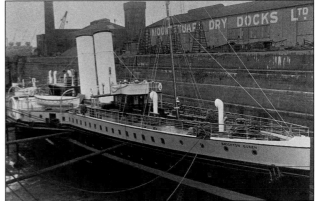

The *Brighton Queen* (formerly the *Lady Moyra*) showing her new name
on 24 May 1933 in the Mountstuart Dry Dock at Avonmouth.
Originally she was the *Gwalia* of the Red Funnel Line.

Bristol Museum

ANY MORE FOR THE *BRIGHTON BELLE*?

For one season only, Campbells experimented with a grey hull for the *Brighton Belle*. She is seen arriving at Weston on 10 July 1937. Instead of admiring the fine lines of the hull, all you want to do is count the portholes; George Owen remarked that she was nicknamed 'The Grey Ghost' for that season... *Bristol Museum*

The little ships, the peace-time excursion steamers, played their part valiantly in the evacuation from Dunkirk. Campbell's *Brighton Belle* was one of the casualties when she struck a submerged wreck and sank. In the best traditions her complement were saved by another paddle steamer, the *Medway Queen* (happily still in existence and being restored in her home waters).

Much moved by this episode of national deliverance and stirred by the paddle steamers' role, Beverley Nichols, the author and journalist, published this poem at the end of the week in the *Sunday Chronicle* of 9 June 1940. Bristol Channel people are proud of their steamers and sentimental about them still; the poem exerts a wistful poignancy these fifty years on.

Any more for the Brighton Belle?
Just two more and we are on our way,
Come on Pa and Ma as well,
It's calm as calm, there ain't no swell,
And what's a bob on holiday.
Any more, any more?
Any more for the Brighton Belle.

A pretty little thing she was, so bright,
Plying the placid waves from shore to shore;
We danced around her decks from morn to night.
And when the music stopped, we called for more.
Whiter than milk the bubbles in her wake,
Brighter than gold the brass upon her rail,
A tiny top upon a painted lake,
When the Belle set sail.

Any more for the Brighton Belle?
Just two more and we are on our way:
Come on Sir, we're off to Hell,
Through a bloody sea to a storm of shell,
Who cares, if we get the boys away!
Any more? Any more for the Brighton Belle.

They came ... in silence, swiftly, faces set,
The little ship received them. All her grace,
Her gaiety, her charm had gone, and yet,
As she set out upon her awful race,
It seemed that music echoed from afar,
It seemed there was a radiance upon the sea,
As though a Voice had drifted from afar,
'Do it to them ... Ye do it unto me,'

Any more for the Brighton Belle?
Come on chum, we're on our way
Bearing the lads who fought and fell,
Out of this hell of shot and shell,
Jerry must wait till another day.
Any more? Any more?
Any more for the Brighton Belle.

The rest is silence, but on that grey sea,
Where drift the ghosts of many an ancient fleet,
No prouder ship has ever sailed than she,
She who could seize such victory from defeat,
And as she sails, (for sail she ever will,
As long as men shall live her tale to tell)
Down the long years the cry will echo still ...
Any more? Any more?
Any more for the Brighton Belle?

PART TWO
WHITE FUNNELS ON THE SOUTH COAST

Talk of White Funnels and the imagination, deeply rooted in historic links, settles instinctively on a stretch of water between Bristol and Lundy Island. Yet, a mere ten years after their arrival in the Bristol Channel, Campbells began, in 1897, a long association with the South Coast.

This enterprise, certainly pictorially, has suffered from some neglect; it has been a pleasure, therefore, to explore the area afresh from the earliest days.

For sixty years, at some stage or another, much of the varied coastline of southern England, from Penzance to Dover, echoed to the beat of Bristol paddles. This remarkable achievement was crowned by the sight of White Funnels, on cross-Channel excursions, in French ports and on occasional forays to the Channel Islands.

The arrival of P. & A. Campbell on the South Coast as a serious competitor to such established fleets as Cosens & Co. and the Southampton, Isle of Wight & South of England Royal Mail Steam Packet Company was a calculated move by the expansion-minded Campbell brothers.

The spring-board for this new development was Queen Victoria's Diamond Jubilee Review of the Fleet on 26 June 1897, for which the *Britannia, Cambria* and *Westward Ho* were despatched, round Land's End, to take part. The *Cambria* was based at Southampton, the *Britannia* and *Westward Ho* at Bournemouth and combined rail and boat trips were advertised in the Western Daily Press. The *Cambria*'s return to the area in August that year for the rest of the season was an indication of the company's confidence.

This superbly animated turn-of-the-century view captures the atmosphere at the end of busy Ryde Pier. Passengers are making their way aboard the *Cambria* for an excursion to Brighton (shown on the destination board behind the bridge). Posters at the barrier advertise sailings of the Southampton & Isle of Wight steamers and the Isle of Wight Central Railway timetable. Significantly an arch-rival, the *Lorna Doone*, is mentioned in bold capitals. The photograph by G. St. John-Biggs of Ryde was taken between 1897 and 1902. Campbells operated many trips from Southampton and Ryde at this period.

Syd Gray

A South Coast presence was put on a permanent footing in the following year, 1898, when Campbells established an office at 71 High Street, Southampton. The *Cambria*, the principal steamer, was joined by the *Glen Rosa*. For the following season, 1899, the *Cambria* ran alone but the *Albion* joined her for the summer of 1900. In 1901 the *Albion* was at Southampton from March to the end of June when she returned to Bristol and the *Cambria* took her place. The *Albion* again went to Southampton at the end of the 1902 August Bank Holiday week, following the stranding of the *Brighton Queen* at Hastings on the Monday.

Despite a reasonably successful début in South Coast waters, the two brothers were looking for a stronger foothold in the excursion business, a niche that they could call their own.

Their objective had been the Brighton, Worthing & South Coast Steam Boat Co. Ltd. and they bought from the liquidators of this troubled concern the *Brighton Queen* and the *Princess May* at the end of February 1902 as a private venture. Their chief prizes were a profitable local station,

Brighton with its two piers, the fast five-year-old paddle steamer *Brighton Queen* and an entrée to a speedier cross-Channel excursion service.

An office was opened at 70 Ship Street, Brighton and the town became the hub of their local sailings. The Southampton station was abandoned at the end of 1902 and, henceforth, it was to Brighton that White Funnel steamers set out from the Bristol Channel at the start of each cruising season.

There were, of course, gaps in services during and after the two world wars but Campbells had found another fiefdom to rule and serve.

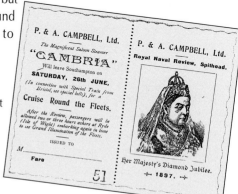

Campbells issued an imposing Review ticket for the *Cambria*'s visit on 26 June, 1897. *George Owen collection*

The promenade at Brighton provides a backdrop for this splendid, formal 1913 group photograph on board the first *Brighton Queen*. The seamen wear distinctive Campbell jerseys; firemen are behind them, while stewards, barmen and galley staff range to the right of the picture.

The Shore Catering Superintendent, Bert Tyrrell, is seated third from the right, with his wife Emily beside him and sister Dorothy on the left. A complement of 38 gives some idea of the necessity for good ship-board management.

The occasion is tinged with sadness; Capt. John West (two rings, seated) died of a heart attack on 4 April, 1914, and the *Brighton Queen* was taken by Capt. McFadyen in her final season.

A splendid picture of the *Brighton Queen* arriving at Brighton, but which pier? The fishing boats in the background might give the answer; possibly the West Pier.

Campbell's *Glen Rosa* (296 grt) sailed from Brighton from 1903 to 1912. She had originally been built for Shearer Brothers of Gourock for their Arran service, on the Clyde, where she plied from 1877 to 1881. The *Glen Rosa* moved to the Thames area, was bought in March 1897 and was chartered by Capt. Alec Campbell to P&A Campbell Ltd., to whom she was sold in 1898. She is seen here to be leaving Brighton on a light run in about 1907.

The *Albion* after her collision with Cosens' *Empress* on 3 May 1901. She is awaiting repairs to her buckled stem at the Northam Iron Works yard, Southampton. Both steamers had come out stern first from Bournemouth Pier, had turned to face each other and the *Albion*'s bow had struck the *Empress* as she went ahead.

George Owen ollection

The Master of the *Albion*, Capt. David James, photographed by W.A. Pelly at Eastbourne, probably in 1913. *H.A. Allen*

Paddle steamers regularly called at the small West Sussex harbour of Littlehampton. Campbell's *Glen Rosa* is seen arriving probably in 1912. At the end of August 1914 she appeared on the Brighton station to relieve the *Ravenswood* which had a cracked cylinder.

Grahame Farr collection

The *Ravenswood* was a South Coast steamer for 1912 to 1914 and this photograph dates from the first of those seasons. Capt. McFadyen (seated centre) has retained several personnel from the old *Bonnie Doon*, including the bandsmen. The picture was taken by W. J. Willmett, the pier photographer at Hastings.

THE ROEDEAN SCHOOL ADVENTURE

The overall pleasure of researching a book like this is sharpened by chance discoveries; an old photograph of the Campbell steamer *Albion* recently came to light. To be honest, I must have had it for years and I certainly don't recall its acquisition. It merely carried the pencilled name 'Roedean', and a question mark, on the reverse.

I vaguely remembered that a paddler had viewed the fleet with a school party just before the First World War, and since there seemed to be a party of girls aboard I could not resist a letter to the school. There is only one 'Roedean'; the famous girls' public school, perched on the cliffs, near Brighton.

A short and very cordial correspondence with the Headmistress, Mrs. Anne Longley, exceeded my greatest hopes; yes, her predecessor had arranged a trip in the summer term of 1914 (probably in May or June, I guess) not just to view but also to visit the First Battle Squadron, comprising H.M. Ships *Collingwood, Hercules, Canterbury*

The pupils of Roedean School, all in uniform and wearing summer boaters, cheerful and disciplined, under the gaze of the staff, pose for the photographer on the *Albion*'s after deck. *Roedean School Archives*

and *Neptune*.

It was a thrilling experience for the girls, who marched down the Palace Pier in double file. The *Albion* had not yet arrived to take the girls to their respective battleships. Youngsters will always make the best of any hiatus; the school magazine reports that 'those who could, possessed themselves of chairs and listened to an orchestra which regaled us with 'tango' tunes, and whiled away the time until word was passed round that the *Albion* had arrived.'

The *Albion* has cast off from Palace Pier with a magnificent frothing of paddle foam. One can almost sense the air of expectancy on board, with the fleet visit ahead.

After their never-to-be-forgotten visit all three hundred and sixty-one Roedean pupils return safely, on the Albion, to Brighton's Palace Pier.
Roedean School Archives

FIRST BATTLE SQUADRON OFF BRIGHTON. 1914. [ROEDEAN ON THE ALBION]

The warships' boats ferried the girls from the *Albion* and, once on board their allotted ship, they divided into parties of six or seven with an officer or a 'middy' for a guided tour. They saw the gun-loading mechanism, examined the searchlight that had blinked at them the previous night, briefly endured the overpowering heat of the engine-room, felt the delicious coolness of the refrigerator room and marvelled that 730 men could live within such a confined space. A few 'adventurous spirits' went down the coal hole, from which they issued forth, the magazine reports, with hands and faces as black as soot!

Each girl received a sailor's hat and a ship's ribbon as a memento of the visit. There was a touching finale for one pupil. In the flurry of departure she lost her boater; it was quickly rescued from the water but had become unwearable. A kindly sailor, seeing her difficulty, gave her his own hat in exchange for the straw boater. No young lady can ever have worn a sailor's hat – back to the waiting motor charabancs – with more pride than she must have done, that afternoon…

The writer of the magazine's report was obviously moved by this naval occasion; 'I should not think that any of us are likely to forget the kindness shown to us as long as we live.'

Subsequently, Roedean presented White Ensigns to the four warships, flags which they took to war just a few months later and which were returned to the school when the ships de-commissioned.

I, too, was moved; that, behind the surface of a rather unremarkable eighty-year-old photograph, I should be able to piece together an intensely human story. Here was youthful excitement, a burst of patriotic sentiment of the kind that would sustain a nation, for all its rights and wrongs, through four years of bitter conflict.

There is also a contemporary message that strides down the decades. Like the *Albion*, that summer's day in 1914, our two remaining large coastal excursion ships, the *Waverley* and the *Balmoral*, still have the power to remind us especially on great nautical occasions that if we lose our maritime heritage a deeply rooted sense of nationhood will also disappear.

The photographs of the ships in this book are inextricably linked with the officers and crews who sailed in them and the passengers of several generations who lined their decks. The social and historical significance of our excursion ships has been, and still is, vastly undervalued.

There was a lapse of four seasons before Campbells resumed their South Coast activities after the First World War. The *Lady Ismay* and the first *Brighton Queen* had been sunk, while the *Albion*, the first *Waverley* and the *Glen Rosa* had been declared unfit for further service.

The loss of five steamers and the process of re-commissioning the rest of their fleet made it prudent for Campbells to concentrate primarily on Bristol Channel sailings. The South Coast would have to wait. Besides, W.H. Tucker of Cardiff had invaded their territory by introducing the *Lady Evelyn*, in June 1919, and the *Lady Moyra* (ex-*Gwalia*). The threat lasted for three seasons, 1919–21, before Campbells were able to absorb both paddlers into their own fleet.

These two useful acquisitions, together with the newly built *Glen Gower*, gave White Funnel the strength to set their sights once more on the South Coast.

During the inter-war years Campbells assigned three paddle steamers to the Brighton station, although there were four in 1936, the little fleet building up as the summer season got under way. The trio for 1923–25 was the *Devonia*, *Brighton Belle* (ex-*Lady Evelyn*) and *Ravenswood*; in the three summers leading up to the Second World War, 1937–39, the *Waverley* (ex-*Barry*), *Brighton Queen* (ex-*Lady Moyra*) and *Glen Gower* were employed. In the intervening years various combinations of these six steamers were used.

The *Westward Ho* also travelled south in 1934 to do a relief at Brighton. Ever watchful for new openings, Campbells based the *Westward Ho* at Plymouth and Torquay in 1932 and 1933 but the experiment was not successful.

An outstanding set of three postcards featuring the *Devonia, Brighton Belle* and *Waverley* was published in about 1926 by Brighton photographers Deane, Wiles and Millar. At his first attempt to photograph the *Devonia* arriving at Brighton the photographer made such a mess of the exposure against the sun that the shadows gave the ship a strange, unflattering hogged profile. The card is reproduced (top left) as an oddity. The lesson was learnt and the subsequent cards showed the *Devonia* and her fleet mates in a far better light.

   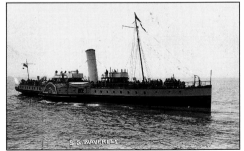

AND SO TO FRANCE...

By the 1900s flourishing English communities were already living and holidaying in the seaside resorts of Northern France. Dinard, opposite St Malo, had an English church, still used by ex-patriates, there was a cliff lift just like Ventnor's and also small paddle steamers.

At Trouville a very English-looking pier took visiting paddlers, Campbells occasionally. Campbell's English Channel Guide (circa 1933) even lists the services of J. V. Parsons, English Chemist, at 24 Rue Victor Hugo, Boulogne; so, no language problems there, while buying perfume or using their Kodak agency.

Day excursions to France are nothing new. Campbells were among the pioneers...a hudred years ago! Fortunately, French publishers like Levy and Stévenard recorded the steamer's visits.

Special STEAMBOAT EXCURSIONS
(Weather & other Circumstances permitting).
SUNDAY, AUGUST 27th. (1911)

11.20 a.m. P.S. "Brighton Queen."	**To BOULOGNE** (Direct) Allowing **4** hours ashore for Casino, etc.	Return Fare, **8/6** CHILDREN, **5/-** Returning from Boulogne 6.15.
10.15 a.m. 5 p.m. (Cheap Trip) P.S. "Waverley."	**To HASTINGS** Leaving Eastbourne Pier } 10.15 a.m. 5 p.m.	Return Fares, **2/-** 5 T Returning from Hastings } 2.40 and 6.
3.40 p.m. P.S. "Waverley."	AFTERNOON CRUISE ROUND **Royal Sovereign Lightship** Back 5 o'clock.	
4.30 p.m. P.S. "Glen Rosa." (Cheap Trip)	**To BRIGHTON** Allowing some time ashore. Returning from Brighton **Palace** Pier 6.40.	Cheap Rail
7.10 p.m. P.S. "Waverley."	EVENING CRUISE OFF **BEXHILL** Back, 8.30.	Fare, **9d.** CHILDREN, 6d.

P. & A. CAMPBELL, Ltd., Pier, Eastbourne.

CHRISTIAN, PRINTER, EASTBOURNE.

No. C 3203 SAISON DE 1927.
P. & A. CAMPBELL Ltd.
CASINO MUNICIPAL DE BOULOGNE-SUR-MER.
Voucher for Special Reduced Admission.
Date 18 AUG 1927 Not Transferable.
Available Date of Issue only.
The Return portion of the Steamboat Ticket must be produced with this Voucher.

One of the lures of Boulogne was the Casino for which Campbells issued a special voucher.

Having reached the shelter of the breakwaters at Boulogne the *Brighton Queen* (1897) does not slacken speed for the long approach to the centre of the town. It might help the reader to note that the first *Brighton Queen*, pre-1914, had only one funnel and the second, a different ship, used from 1933, had two.

Between the ports of Dieppe and Le Havre lies the town of Fécamp. The local Chamber of Commerce, in conjunction with the French Tourist Board in London, arranged a special trip on 22 July 1935. This photograph of the second *Brighton Queen*'s arrival at Fécamp must rank as one of the rarest studies of a White Funnel steamer in a French port.

Lionel Vaughan

Heavily laden with day trippers the *Brighton Queen* paddles past the railway steamers berthed beside the Gare Maritime on the south side of Boulogne harbour.

E. S. BOULOGNE-sur-MER
Le " Devonia ", Bateau d'Excursions France-Angleterre

Passengers for Boulogne enjoyed a very good summer service between the wars with up to four trips a week. The *Devonia*, pictured here in her first or second season (1923 or 1924) would normally start her day with calls at the two Brighton piers, thence to Eastbourne and Hastings, before crossing to the French port. There were two to three hours ashore and the return to the Sussex coast was in reverse order.

An interesting inter-war study of the *Waverley* (ex-*Barry*) canting at Calais.
H. A Allen

WHITE FUNNEL FLEET

SPECIAL EXCURSION from BRISTOL, CARDIFF and ILFRACOMBE

TO

BRIGHTON

AND BACK.

(Weather and circumstances permitting) by the Magnificent Saloon Steamer

"GLEN GOWER"

On TUESDAY, 31st AUGUST, 1926

Leaving Bristol (Hotwells) 12.0 noon, Cardiff 2.15 p.m., Penarth 2.25 p.m, Ilfracombe 4 45 p.m., due at Brighton on the Evening of Wednesday, September 1st, returning by the

"DEVONIA"

On FRIDAY, 3rd SEPTEMBER, 1926

Leaving Brighton (West Pier) at 9.30 a.m., due to arrive at Ilfracombe, Saturday morning and leave at 2.0 p.m., Penarth 4.10 p.m., Cardiff 4 35 p.m., Clevedon 5.35 p.m., due at Bristol about 6.30 p.m. on Saturday, September 4th.

Single Fare, 15/-   Special Return Fare, 21/-

BOAT AND RAIL FACILITIES

enabling passengers travelling outwards by Steamer to return by Rail within 15 days.

RETURN FARES (Out by Boat, Home by Rail).

	BRISTOL.	CARDIFF.	ILFRACOMBE.
To or from BRIGHTON	30/-	35/-	40/-
To or from WORTHING	31/-	36/6	40/-
To or from EASTBOURNE	37/-	42/-	49/6
To or from HASTINGS	40/-	44/6	51/6

The journeys to or from Brighton and Bristol or Cardiff may be made either via London or Salisbury; to or from Ilfracombe by the Salisbury and Southern Co. route only; those to or from Eastbourne or Hastings via London only; those to or from Worthing by the Salisbury and Southern route only. In the cases of Worthing, Eastbourne and Hastings, the fares include the outward or return journey to or from Brighton.

Return Fare includes Third Class Rail and the rail portions of the tickets are available to return up to and including Sept. 13th and Sept. 17th respectively by any train carrying third-class passengers.

Tickets obtainable from Messrs. Thos. Cook & Son, Ltd., at the following offices :—81 Kings Road, Brighton; 23, Baldwin Street, Bristol; or 28, High Street, Cardiff; or on board Steamer.

Agents of P. & Campbell, Ltd., Cumberland Basin, Bristol:—Wm. Guy, 1, Stuart Street, Cardiff; F. W. Birmingham, 10, The Quay, Ilfracombe; W. Reid, 7, Old Steine, Brighton; W. A. Pelly, Pier, Eastbourne; F. L. Phillips, Pier, Hastings.

Dates, Ltd., Printers, Cardiff.

The year 1926 was a difficult one for all steamship owners; it was the year of the General Strike and Campbells suffered, like everyone else, from diminished coal supplies and lack of quality. The *Devonia* was heavy on coal and the decision was taken to replace her on the South Coast with the *Glen Gower* for the final month of the season.

Although she was not destined to return to these waters until 1934 to 1939, this was the *Glen Gower*'s Brighton début. Happy to reap some reward from the positioning run the company offered a superb late summer bonus to the adventurous; out from Bristol by the *Glen Gower* on Tuesday, 31 August and back by the *Devonia* on the Friday from Brighton. Immediate or period returns were alternative parts of the package. A poster of some rarity catalogues the fares for this remarkable trip.

Campbell's second *Brighton Queen* (519 grt) had started her life on the Bristol Channel as the Barry Railway Co's *Gwalia* in 1905, passing to the Furness Railway Co. in 1910. She spent three seasons for other Bristol Channel owners and then joined the White Funnel Fleet in 1922. The paddler retained her Furness name, *Lady Moyra*, until 1933 when she arrived on the South Coast as the *Brighton Queen*. She is pictured, here, in her first season on the South Coast, leaving Eastbourne in September 1933.

Bristol Museum

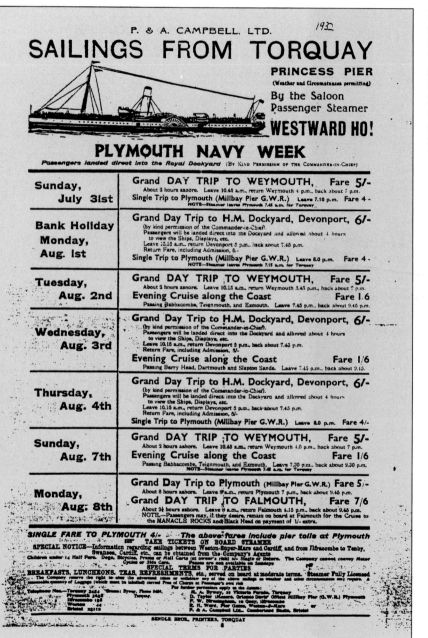

P. & A. CAMPBELL. LTD.

193?

SAILINGS FROM TORQUAY

PRINCESS PIER
(Weather and Circumstances permitting)

By the Saloon
Passenger Steamer

WESTWARD HO!

PLYMOUTH NAVY WEEK

Passengers landed direct into the Royal Dockyard (By Kind Permission of the Commander-in-Chief)

Sunday, July 31st	**Grand DAY TRIP TO WEYMOUTH, Fare 5/-** About 2 hours ashore. Leave 10.45 a.m., return Weymouth 4 p.m., back about 7 p.m. Single Trip to Plymouth (Millbay Pier G.W.R.) Leave 7.10 p.m. Fare 4/- NOTE—Steamer leaves Plymouth 7.45 a.m. for Torquay
Bank Holiday Monday, Aug. 1st	**Grand Day Trip to H.M. Dockyard, Devonport, 6/-** (by kind permission of the Commander-in-Chief) Passengers will be landed direct into the Dockyard and allowed about 4 hours to view the Ships, Displays, etc. Leave 10.15 a.m., return Devonport 5 p.m., back about 7.45 p.m. Return Fare, including Admission, 6/- Single Trip to Plymouth (Millbay Pier G.W.R.) Leave 8.0 p.m. Fare 4/-
Tuesday, Aug. 2nd	**Grand DAY TRIP TO WEYMOUTH, Fare 5/-** About 2 hours ashore. Leave 10.15 a.m., return Weymouth 3.45 p.m., back about 7 p.m. **Evening Cruise along the Coast Fare 1/6** Passing Babbacombe, Teignmouth, and Exmouth. Leave 7.45 p.m. back about 9.45 p.m.
Wednesday, Aug. 3rd	**Grand Day Trip to H.M. Dockyard, Devonport, 6/-** (by kind permission of the Commander-in-Chief) Passengers will be landed direct into the Dockyard and allowed about 4 hours to view the Ships, Displays, etc. Leave 10.15 a.m., return Devonport 5 p.m., back about 7.45 p.m. Return Fare, including Admission, 6/- **Evening Cruise along the Coast Fare 1/6** Passing Berry Head, Dartmouth and Slapton Sands. Leave 7.45 p.m., back about 9.45.
Thursday, Aug. 4th	**Grand Day Trip to H.M. Dockyard, Devonport, 6/-** (by kind permission of the Commander-in-Chief) Passengers will be landed direct into the Dockyard and allowed about 4 hours to view the Ships, Displays, etc. Leave 10.15 a.m., return Devonport 5 p.m., back about 7.45 p.m. Return Fare, including Admission, 6/- Single Trip to Plymouth (Millbay Pier G.W.R.) Leave 8.0 p.m. Fare 4/-
Sunday, Aug. 7th	**Grand DAY TRIP TO WEYMOUTH, Fare 5/-** About 2 hours ashore. Leave 10.45 a.m., return Weymouth 4.0 p.m., back about 7 p.m. **Evening Cruise along the Coast Fare 1/6** Passing Babbacombe, Teignmouth, and Exmouth. Leave 7.30 p.m., back about 9.30 p.m. NOTE—Steamer leaves Plymouth 7.45 a.m. for Torquay
Monday, Aug. 8th	**Grand Day Trip to Plymouth (Millbay Pier G.W.R.) Fare 5/-** About 8 hours ashore. Leave 9 a.m., return Plymouth 7 p.m., back about 9.45 p.m. **Grand DAY TRIP TO FALMOUTH, Fare 7/6** About 3½ hours ashore. Leave 8 a.m., return Falmouth 4.15 p.m., back about 9.45 p.m. NOTE.—Passengers may, if they desire, remain on board at Falmouth for the Cruise to the MANACLE ROCKS and Black Head on payment of 1/- extra.

SINGLE FARE TO PLYMOUTH 4/- *The above fares include pier tolls at Plymouth*
☞ **TAKE TICKETS ON BOARD STEAMER**

SPECIAL NOTICE—Information regarding sailings between Weston-Super-Mare and Cardiff, and from Ilfracombe to Tenby, Swansea, Cardiff, etc., can be obtained from the Company's Agents
Children under 14 Half Fare. Dogs, Bicycles, Prams or Mail Carts (at owner's risk) on Single or Return. The Company cannot convey Motor Cycles or Side Cars. Passes are not available on Sundays

SPECIAL TERMS FOR PARTIES

BREAKFASTS, LUNCHEONS, TEAS, REFRESHMENTS, etc., served on board at moderate terms. Steamer Fully Licensed
The Company reserve the right to alter the advertised times or withdraw any of the above sailings as weather and other circumstances may require. A quantity of Luggage (which must be labelled) carried Free of Charge at Passenger's own risk

For further particulars apply to the Agents:
Telephone Nos.—Torquay 3434 'Grams: Byway, Phone 3434.
Plymouth 3415 Torquay.
Ilfracombe 125
Weston 44
Bristol 25112

M. A. Byway, 27 Victoria Parade, Torquay
D. Taylor (Messrs. Orianne Davey Office) Millbay Pier (G.W.R.) Plymouth
F. W. Birmingham, 10 Quay, Ilfracombe
R. H. Ward, Pier Gates, Weston-s-Mare
P. & A. Campbell Ltd., Cumberland Basin, Bristol

BENDLE BROS., PRINTERS, TORQUAY

In 1932 and 1933 the *Westward Ho* was based at Torquay and Plymouth. The 1932 handbill for the beginning of August shows the *Westward Ho* leaving Princess Pier, Torquay, at 10.15 a.m. for a 'Grand Day Trip to H.M. Dockyard, Devonport' on Bank Holiday Monday 1 August and again on the Wednesday and Thursday. Passengers were landed in the dockyard at 1.00 p.m. for four hours 'to view the ships, displays, etc.' before returning to Torquay — the fare, six shillings.

George Owen collection

Campbells ran special excursions to Plymouth Navy Week. The *Westward Ho* is pictured in the Hamoaze of the River Tamar on one of these occasions in 1932 or 1933. The distinctive landmark of the twin stacks of Devonport Dockyard's engineering complex, the Quadrangle, can be seen on the right.

The *Westward Ho* is seen here approaching the Prince of Wales Pier at Falmouth during her 1932 or 1933 season. Local memory recalls her as the largest excursion ship ever to call at the pier, which reportedly shook as she bumped alongside. The sailing ship in the background is the *Cutty Sark*, which was anchored there until 1938.

George Owen collection

"WESTWARD HO" LEAVING FOWEY.

The *Westward Ho* looks fairly busy as she leaves Fowey on an excursion; a photograph from the 1932 or 1933 season.

Alan Kittridge

A rare photograph of the *Westward Ho* moored at the outer breakwater of Mevagissey.

Victor Keen

"BRIGHTON QUEEN" ILFRACOMBE 1934 on "Round the Land Trip"

Sid Partington combined the duties of Purser and Radio Officer on the South Coast between the wars. The photo is from 1933.

Dorothy Partington

The *Brighton Queen* has briefly put into Ilfracombe before departing her long haul round Land's End for the 1934 Brighton season. The officers have been assembled for a farewell snapshot with Johnny Black, Chief Engineer, on the left of the group. One can only speculate on the photographer's instructions. Perhaps, 'Relax, look cheerful and, all of you, try to do something different with your hands!' Capt. Couves, on the right, has responded with his customary good humour.

The day was Thursday, 21 June and the *Brighton Queen* left at 4.15 p.m.; passengers from Ilfracombe were due to arrive on their circular trip (back by train) at Palace Pier, Brighton at 3 p.m. on Friday. Earlier, on that Thursday morning, the *Waverley* left Bristol (11.40 a.m.), calling at Clevedon and Weston, to connect with the *Brighton Queen* at Ilfracombe and there were other passengers by another steamer from Cardiff and Minehead.

On a personal note, it is a great thrill for an author to be given a photograph like this, to research it and to savour the suppressed anticipation on board, the excitement of a trip about to take place sixty years ago. The return fare from Cardiff to Brighton was 35 shillings.

Syd Gray

The Brighton station was reopened in 1947, first by the *Glen Gower* which was replaced in July by the turbine steamer *Empress Queen*. The *Empress Queen* and the *Britannia* represented Campbells there for the seasons of 1948 and 1949, while in 1950 the *Glen Gower* was on the South Coast for a short spell until relieved by the *Empress Queen*.

An interesting experiment was tried in 1951; Brighton was abandoned and the *Empress Queen* was sent to Torquay to open up a new service to Guernsey; she also made some trips to Alderney. Grahame Farr records that her first trip to Guernsey was on 25 June, that she had good sea-going qualities but that her passenger capacity – 1,300 for shorter cruises – could not be economically used. It was a brave attempt to find the kind of excursions which could support a ship of this size, denied as she was the route to France for which she had originally been intended.

The Torquay venture was not a success and the *Empress Queen* was laid up in the Centre, Bristol; a rather tragic fate, for she never sailed for Campbells again. The *Cardiff Queen* was chosen to go to Brighton during the 1952 and 1953 seasons, and from 1954 to 1956 it was the *Glen Gower*'s turn.

Eddie Wood, now of Winterbourne near Bristol, was one of the last generation of South Coast pursers. Eddie served on the *Britannia* in the Bristol Channel and also south with the *Cardiff Queen*. 'I was Eastbourne Agent in 1957; Mr. McDougall was Agent at Brighton and Mr. McNair was at Hastings.'

In time-honoured tradition, Eddie and his wife and family took accommodation in Brighton for the season; 'We had a flat opposite the pier. One day the chap in the flat below came up to complain about the noise our children made in the early morning. We told him about the row from his late night parties. After that we got on fine. It was Sandy Powell, the entertainer.'

Campbell's final chapter on the South Coast was written almost as an epilogue. The *Glen Gower* had suffered grievously from the weather in 1956; a total of 23 sailing days had been lost, Grahame Farr reported, including 17 cross-channel excursions. The *Glen Gower* spent her final season on the Bristol Channel, in 1957, principally on the Cardiff-Weston run.

Mindful of the need for economy Campbells chartered the small motorship *Crested Eagle* in 1957; she had become surplus to the services of the General Steam Navigation Company. Her season with Campbells, according to Roy Barclay, her Second Engineer, was dogged by engine problems; 'We were always repairing the engines at night and ended up by renaming her the Ruptured Bird,' he said ruefully.

The *Crested Eagle*, based at Newhaven (Pier 13), spent most of her time between Eastbourne and Hastings; twice a week she called at Brighton and once a week extended to Shanklin. Her final trip on Sunday, 29 September 1957, marked the end of White Funnel cruising on the South Coast on a regular basis, though the charmed career of the *Balmoral* was destined to show the Campbell house-flag on the South Coast occasionally in later years.

There was, however, an interesting postscript. In the early days of their growth, Townsend, the pioneer ferry company,

relied heavily on Campbells to promote its cross-Channel excursions. Campbells' Eastbourne office reopened in 1965, Hastings and Brighton in 1966, new offices opened at Margate, Ramsgate, Deal and Southend in 1967, Bournemouth and Southsea in 1968 and Bognor (1969 only). Peter Southcombe, who helped set up and administer this new initiative re-inforced the point, 'Townsend's whole south and south east coast excursion effort was planned, operated and administered by Campbells until the end of the 1971 season. The only thing they did not have was the ships, except for the *Queen of the Isles*, on charter, in 1969.'

All aboard, at Brighton! A super boarding scene of the *Empress Queen* in 1950 a fine selection of watchers, leaners and queuers.

H.A. Allen

The *Empress Queen*, moored at Torquay in 1951. It is the same berth subsequently used by the *Devoniun*, formerly Campbell's motor-ship *Devonia*, in her days with Torbay Seaways Ltd. *Edwin R. Keen*

A magnificent photograph of the *Empress Queen* arriving at St Peter Port, Guernsey. This was the turbine steamer's maiden trip to the island from Torquay, on 25 June 1951. There were 198 passengers on board.

The Guernsey Press

THE CORONATION REVIEW

The last time that P. & A. Campbell were represented in force on the South Coast was at the Coronation Review, Spithead, in 1953. Three steamers were in attendance: the *Bristol Queen* (chartered by English Electric), the *Cardiff Queen* (Frames Tours) and the *Glen Gower* (chartered by Dean and Dawson).

For days in advance of 15 June the fine, natural anchorage between Portsmouth and the approach to Southampton Water had filled with a magnificent armada of fighting ships of the Royal Navy. Visiting foreign warships and a representative cross-section of the British Merchant Marine – from ocean liners like the *Uganda* (British India S.N.Co.) to small coasters like the *Milo* (Bristol Steam Navigation Co.) – added a uniquely cosmopolitan flavour to the event.

The lines were joined, on the morning of the Review, by many coastal excursion steamers, whose decks provided

SNR 8　　THE CORONATION NAVAL REVIEW AT SPITHEAD　　A TUCK CARD
THE QUEEN ON BOARD THE ROYAL YACHT "SURPRISE"

The Queen is welcomed aboard HMS *Surprise* by Vice-Admiral Sir Conolly Abel Smith (Flag Officer Royal Yacht). The young Surgeon Lieutenant – now Dr. Tony Pilkington – whom Her Majesty has just passed, remembers the day well; 'Unfortunately it was pouring with rain, so we had to keep the canopy up.'

E ɪɪ R
1953

HER MAJESTY'S
CORONATION NAVAL REVIEW
AT SPITHEAD

p.s. Bristol Queen, 15th June 1953

A special train left Waterloo for Southampton Docks at 7.45 a.m. The *Bristol Queen* is pictured at Berth No. 38, where her passengers embarked. She left for the anchorage at 9.50. A preview had already been staged by the *Bristol Queen* two days before, with Bristolians travelling via Bath (Green Park) and Blandford, down the Somerset and Dorset line, to Southampton.

Syd Gray

a superb grandstand for invited guests and general public to watch H.M. Queen Elizabeth review her navy from HMS *Surprise*, Royal Yacht for the occasion.

The Campbell paddlers were in excellent company. Anchored at the lower end of Southampton Water were the *Consul*, *Embassy*, *Monarch* and *Emperor of India* (Cosens & Co.Ltd); *Bournemouth Queen*, *Medina*, *Princess Elizabeth*, *Balmoral* and *Vecta* (Southampton & Isle of Wight RMSP Co.Ltd). On the south side of the anchorage, off Ryde Pier, were the *Farringford*, *Whippingham*, *Ryde* and *Freshwater* (British Railways, Southern Region); the *Royal Daffodil*, *Royal Sovereign* and *Medway Queen* (General Steam Navigation Co.Ltd). The *Southsea* and *Brading* (British Railways) were anchored off Horse Sand Fort next to HMS *Vanguard*, the pride of the fleet.

Within a mere twenty years the regular excursion services of these seaside favourites had passed into history.

See the NAVAL REVIEW from the "CARDIFF QUEEN"

Come with us! See this magnificent height-of-summer pageant of the sea! Nearly two hundred Royal Navy ships of every size and description will be there, with Commonwealth and foreign ships, merchant ships and many others.

Her Majesty the Queen sets sail this June Monday, accompanied by the Duke of Edinburgh, to review the vast and powerful assemblage of warships and see the magnificent fly-past of hundreds of naval aircraft.

The Coronation Naval Review is an outstanding event: the naval occasion of a whole reign. This is your life-time opportunity to be there, amidst the hundreds of ships and to get a really close-range view of the greatest variety of modern vessels ever assembled on one naval-ground—aircraft-carriers, cruisers, destroyers, frigates, submarines as well as all types of other ships from large ocean liners to small coastal craft and private yachts.

Come with us! We have chartered the oil-fired *Cardiff Queen* (Capt. E. C. Phillips, D.S.C.). This is the newest (1947) steamer of the excellent fleet of P. & A. Campbell Ltd., noted for their superior catering.

Your comfort is assured. Only 450 persons will be booked for this sailing—the *Cardiff Queen* is licensed for 1,000 persons. There are excellent bars on board, also a buffet where light refreshments are obtainable at reasonable prices at all times. Well-appointed dining saloons and a ladies' retiring room form part of this vessel's bright interior. There is ample open-air seating and generous covered accommodation. There will also be a travel enquiry bureau on board, and the official Naval Review programme will be on sale.

Admiralty permission has been requested for the *Cardiff Queen* to cruise through the naval lines to give you close-range views. Being a paddle steamer, the *Cardiff Queen* is extremely manoeuvrable in a busy anchorage. A running commentary, with intervals of light music, will inform and entertain.

At night, a glittering maze of illuminations and fireworks will add the final note of festivity to this rare and glorious event.

The Inclusive Fare of
£12 12s. 0d. *Provides:*
1. Travel by special train London to Southampton and back.
2. Cruise to Spithead, and view of naval inspection by Her Majesty.
3. Table d'hote luncheon and supper on board.
4. Cruise around the Fleet, subject to Admiralty permission.
5. View of Illuminations, searchlight display and fireworks.

No reduction for children.

Provisional Programme

Some of these details are based on the corresponding arrangements made for the 1937 review. Exact details are expected towards the end of March. In the meantime, however, it is desirable to book your places in this limited cruise.

Monday, June 15th. Leave London (Waterloo Station) by special train about 8 a.m. (exact time will be confirmed later).

Shortly after arrival of the train at Southampton the *Cardiff Queen* will depart, passing many of the great and famous passenger ships which dock there, and will cruise through the Fleet to her specially reserved anchorage.

About 2 p.m. the Queen, accompanied by The Duke of Edinburgh and members of the Admiralty, proceeds to Spithead.

About 4 p.m. the Queen inspects the Fleet, and at the end of the Review the Fleet Air Arm will fly past.

About 6 p.m. the *Cardiff Queen* will, subject to Admiralty permission, leave her anchorage and cruise through the naval lines, and from 10 p.m. to midnight the Fleet will be illuminated and will give a searchlight and firework display.

Arrive at Southampton after midnight. Special train departs for London (Waterloo) arriving early morning.

P.S. "Cardiff Queen"   (Length 247 ft., Beam 60 ft., Speed 17½ knots)   Photo: J. Holt.

PREVIOUS NAVAL REVIEW SUCCESSES

In 1935 and 1937 we chartered Messrs. P. & A. Campbell's flagship of that time. Following are some letters we received:

"I must congratulate your firm on the way you carried out the Naval Review tour. Everything was so comfortable and so well arranged. I enjoyed every moment."
(Lady) M.F.-W.

"A most happy time. A more delightful set of people we could not have wished to sail with."—S.C.W.

"Congratulations to all, and not least to the Captain, and to Commander Badger, the interesting commentator. Splendid opportunity of seeing the Fleet at close quarters . . . a perfect day."—(Miss) V.M.

"Our office has received a number of calls from passengers who expressed satisfaction with the cruise."—letter from a booking office.

Luncheon Menu

Fruit Juices
Tomato Soup
or
Consommé Julienne
Cold Salmon
or
Cold Meats
or
Cold Veal and Ham Pie
Potatoes
Salads

Apple Tarts and Custard
Compote of Fruit
Prunes and Creamed Rice

Biscuits and Cheese

Catering

The *Cardiff Queen* is the newest ship of a line that takes pride in its catering and service.

Besides the main meals which are provided, there will be tea and cakes available at any time at normal prices, and the bars will be open throughout the day.

SITTINGS FOR MEALS

When booking, please state the sitting you prefer:
1st sitting:
    luncheon 11-30, supper 6-0.
2nd sitting:
    luncheon 12-30, supper 7-0.
3rd sitting:
    luncheon 1-30, supper 8-0.

Supper Menu

Cold Meat
Salad
or
Fried Fillets of Plaice
Fried Fillets of Sole
or
Cold Salmon
Chipped or Boiled Potatoes
Bread and Butter

Preserves

Biscuits and Cheese

Tea or Coffee

Photo—Broadhead   A Dining Saloon and Bar of the *Cardiff Queen*.   Photo—Crosely

To-day there is one historic survivor from that list, still actively engaged in traditional pleasure trips; the *Balmoral* now operated by Waverley Excursions Ltd. has happily outlasted them all.

The Royal Yacht Britannia had still to be completed so the Royal Party embarked at South Railway Pier, Portsmouth, on HMS *Surprise*, which acted as Royal Yacht for the occasion. Casting off at 3 o'clock, HMS *Surprise* entered the lines an hour later when Her Majesty Queen Elizabeth II reviewed the Fleet.

It was the turn of the excursion ships to pass down the lines between 6pm and 10pm. Rarely can the *Bristol Queen*, immaculate and dressed overall, have made such a dramatic cruise. For the select gathering on board it was the trip of a lifetime. The illumination of the Fleet and the grand firework finale were still to come. The memorable day came to a close just after midnight when the *Bristol Queen* weighed anchor for the short return trip to Southampton; the waiting train was scheduled to arrive at Waterloo at 3.40am as dawn began to break over the slumbering capital.

The *Bristol Queen*'s guest list for the Spithead Review read like a Who's Who of British industry, drawn in particular from the nationalised spheres of coal, electricity, steel and telecommunications. There was a sprinkling of foreign diplomats and industrial 'opposite numbers' while the only genuine Bristolians appeared to be Sir Reginald and Lady Verdon Smith, representing the Bristol Aeroplane Co.

Syd Gray

69

The winter of 1962–63 brought icy conditions to the Dorset coast, and indeed to much of the south. The *Bristol Queen* broke new ground by going to Weymouth for her overhaul and repainting.

Two fine photographs capture a low and high point in the cruising calendar. The first, in the very depths of hibernation, is a wonderfully atmospheric study of that between-seasons moment when the spirit of carefree summer trips is furthest from the mind. The other picture, just a few weeks forward, carries with it all the optimism of a new season ahead and the heady expectations of a glorious summer.

These two pictures mirror perfectly what the heart and soul of cruising enthusiasts instinctively feel when not on board. Winter is for memories, slides and photographs; spring brings a surge of fresh hope and optimism.

Left: Weymouth waterfront is under a mantle of snow. The funnels and upper-works of the *Bristol Queen* look uncharacteristically grey beneath a leaden sky. *Geoff Pritchard*

Below: It's spring again – May 1963 – and the *Bristol Queen*, under tow, emerges stern-first from the inner harbour in the tricky manoeuvre through Weymouth's fine bascule bridge. *Paul Webb collection*

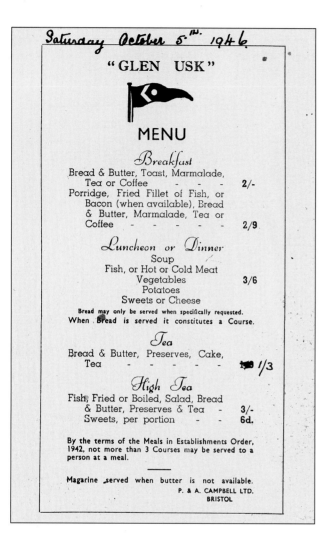

Saturday October 5th. 1946.

"GLEN USK"

MENU

Breakfast

Bread & Butter, Toast, Marmalade, Tea or Coffee	2/-
Porridge, Fried Fillet of Fish, or Bacon (when available), Bread & Butter, Marmalade, Tea or Coffee	2/9

Luncheon or Dinner

Soup
Fish, or Hot or Cold Meat   3/6
Vegetables
Potatoes
Sweets or Cheese

Bread may only be served when specifically requested.
When Bread is served it constitutes a Course.

Tea

Bread & Butter, Preserves, Cake, Tea	1/3

High Tea

Fish, Fried or Boiled, Salad, Bread & Butter, Preserves & Tea	3/-
Sweets, per portion	6d.

By the terms of the Meals in Establishments Order, 1942, not more than 3 Courses may be served to a person at a meal.

Margarine served when butter is not available.

P. & A. CAMPBELL LTD.
BRISTOL

The passage of time tends to eclipse the severity of post-war restrictions on luxuries like fuel and sweets. Even necessities such as clothing and food were rationed.

A printed menu from the *Glen Usk*'s 1946 season gives a fascinating account of what you were allowed to eat (if available...)

Saturday 5 October, the date on the menu, was also the occasion of the *Glen Usk*'s farewell, end of season dinner for officers and crew. These tended to be very lively affairs and signing of menus was a happy tradition. There are some well known Campbell names on the reverse, Capts. McLean Shedden and Albert Murphy, Tommy Price (Chief Engineer), Mr Dunning (Chief Steward), and Bill Forbes, (Purser) among them.

Syd Gray

PART THREE
WHITE FUNNELS IN THE BRISTOL CHANNEL
1946–1980

Summer seems an age away from this mid-winter snow scene. Britain froze in 1947 and the *Bristol Queen*'s decks are covered in a thick mantle of white as she lies at her lay-up berth in Bristol, next to the Flying Fox. The railway tracks in the foreground ran up Hotwells to the timber wharf, the coke terminal and the busy sheds which are now part of the Exhibition Centre.   *Syd Gray*

THE SAD EMPRESS

The *Empress Queen* (1,781 grt) enjoyed a pitifully short peace-time career between 1947 and 1951. She may have been a turbine steamer but Campbell's paddler tradition could not have been broken by a finer-looking ship. It is significant that the Clyde had seen turbine steamers since the introduction of the *King Edward* in 1901, a tradition which ended with the *Queen Mary*, withdrawn in 1977. It was the misfortune of the *Empress Queen* to be a much bigger ship than her Clyde counterparts and, therefore, unsuitable for coastal cruising. Had the war not intervened she would have had an assured future on the South Coast; instead, she became a costly encumbrance and contributed to Campbell's post-war financial problems. It really was a paradox that such a beautiful vessel could, unwittingly, have caused so much financial heartache.

After her war service the *Empress Queen* went back to her builders, the Ailsa Shipbuilding Co., Troon. In this unusual photograph she is seen during the refit early in 1947 in Troon harbour.　*Lin Bryant collection*

This extremely rare artist's impression shows a good likeness, if not quite capturing the flared sweep of the bows. The *Empress Queen* bears a distinct resemblance to the kind of small turbine ships such as the *Tynwald* (built 1937) of the Isle of Man Steam Packet Company then being envisaged for a combination of excursions and short-sea passenger crossings.

It was a brave decision for Campbells to order the *Empress Queen* with an eye to their South Coast cross-channel service, a vision so cruelly thwarted by the outbreak of war. The return to the company of the *Empress Queen* at the end of hostilities, combined with the passport restrictions which denied her a satisfactory role on the South Coast, helped to compound Campbell's post-war problems

P. & A. CAMPBELL LTD.
ARTISTS IMPRESSION
NEW LUXURY TURBINE CROSS CHANNEL STEAMER

This attractive view of Campbell's turbine steamer *Empress Queen* was taken on the Clyde on 16 June 1947 following her extensive post-war refit at Troon. George Owen makes an interesting comment that the *Empress Queen* is carrying the 'A' flag at the foremast head to indicate AM ON FULL SPEED TRIALS, KEEP CLEAR.

After the rigours of war this was a wonderful moment. Dressed overall, the *Empress Queen* left Swansea on 27 June 1947 on an evening cruise which was her maiden trip in peacetime. The following day she made her first trip to Ilfracombe.   *George Owen*

Interior photographs of the *Empress Queen* are a rarity. This shows part of her dining saloon on 22 August, 1954, while she was awaiting a buyer.   *Syd Gray*

A rare photograph of the *Empress Queen* at Ilfracombe. She was not very manoeuvrable in restricted waters. Close scrutiny reveals that the anchor stock is not in the hawse-pipe but has been driven through the plating. This occurred on the afternoon of 1 July, 1947 when the *Empress Queen* hit a pile at Ilfracombe.

Dorothy Partington

The *Empress Queen* photographed in the Cumberland Basin, Bristol.
Jim Fraser

In steam, but under tow for her last trip down the Avon, Campbell's *Empress Queen* leaves Bristol for Greece on 3 April 1955. Photographed at the Horseshoe Bend her new name, *Philippos*, is visible at the bow; below decks, and thankfully unseen, was a consignment of lavatory pans. *Grahame Farr collection*

There is no mistaking the former Campbell's turbine steamer *Empress Queen*. Greek-owned by the Kavounides Shipping Co. as the *Philippos*, she is seen here at Venice sometime after 1955. *Eric Payne*

THE FINNISH BARQUE "PASSAT" ARRIVING IN
PENARTH ROADS ON HER LAST VOYAGE FROM
AUSTRALIA. THE P.S. "GLEN USK" PASSING
ASTERN.

PHOTOGRAPH BY COURTESY OF THE
DOCKS & INLAND WATERWAYS EXECUTIVE
(SOUTH WALES DOCKS)

With the Compliments of
P & A · Campbell Ltd
1 BRITANNIA BLDGS · CUMBERLAND BASIN
BRISTOL · 8
TEL. 23112

PASSENGER STEAMSHIP
OWNERS

The end of an era. The magnificent four-masted barque *Passat* made two commercial trips to the Bristol Channel with grain from Australia. On the first occasion she came to Avonmouth in October 1948 and I have a vivid recollection of her stately passage up, past Portishead.

On 4 October 1949 the *Passat* was towed into Penarth for discharge. She was one of the last square-riggers to be thus employed. The *Glen Usk* is seen passing astern of her in Penarth Roads. What an unforgettable experience it must have been for the *Glen Usk*'s passengers! Campbell's subsequently used the picture as their calendar feature.

A quiet moment, at anchor in 1949 off Ilfracombe; Jimmy Martin, a long-serving Campbell's Chief Officer, and Capt. Albert Murphy (right).

James Martin had served in the Red Funnel steamers, joining Campbells when they took over. During the First World War he was decorated for using a hammer and chisel to cut loose a mine which had come up, badly tangled in the sweep. George Owen remembers him as Mate with Capt. Fred Nunn in the *Lady Moyra* during 1927 and the *Glen Gower* from 1928 until 1932; and as Mate with Capt. J.A. Harris in the *Glen Gower* from 1933 until she went round to the south coast in 1934, when he transferred to the *Cambria*.

'My next memory of James Martin was as Mate in the *Glen Gower* (1948-9) with Capt. Albert Murphy. Both Officers went to the *Cardiff Queen* for 1950 and 1951, when I think he must have retired,' George Owen recalled. 'He was a prime seaman and a great 'character'.'

It was a truly remarkable career which spanned almost fifty years of Bristol Channel steamer history. It is profoundly disturbing that such an opportunity to serve has disappeared from what is left of our diminishing Merchant Service. *Syd Gray*

The *Glen Usk* high and dry alongside Newport pontoon in 1954. The photograph emphasises the enormous tidal range of the Bristol Channel's river estuaries. It helps to put into perspective the complex timetabling which was required, the tides being roughly one hour later each successive day.

Grahame Farr collection

Two splendid deck views of the *Glen Usk*. Looking aft from the bow and (below) looking forward, Birnbeck Pier and Weston Bay are fast approaching.

Trevor Morgan

The *Glen Gower* makes an attractive picture as she arrives at Penarth in the fifties.

Trevor Morgan

P.S. *Britannia's*
Farewell Cruise to Ilfracombe

Wednesday, September 19th
1956

P. and A. Campbell Ltd.
CUMBERLAND BASIN · BRISTOL

WHITE FUNNEL

In the fifties the *Britannia* was still a mainstay of the long-distance excursions from Bristol. She was roomy, still had a good turn of speed with her new boilers and provided that pre-war link with cruising tradition that made her a Bristol favourite – after all, having been built in 1896, she went back to the very roots of the Campbell dynasty.

The *Britannia* is setting off down the River Avon. The Clifton Suspension Bridge provides a wonderful vantage point.   *Jim Fraser*

It was a great blow when it was decided to withdraw the faithful *Britannia* in 1956. The Bristol Evening World chartered the 'Old Brit.' for a farewell cruise from Bristol to Ilfracombe on 19 September, 1956. She did, in fact, win a week's reprieve to deputise for the *Glen Usk* on the Weston ferry, running her final trips on 26 September. The demise of this popular paddle steamer was much regretted.   *Syd Gray*

An unusual photographic point in Bristol's Floating Harbour was the South Side, over by the timber yards. The *Cardiff Queen* is moored on the Hotwells Road with the *Glen Gower* in the foreground. This tranquil scene is probably just pre-season in the fifties, as both ships look to have been freshly painted – none of those waterline streaks or fairlead rust so characteristic of the winter lay-up period.

Jim Fraser

Underfall Yard was the heart of Campbells' overhaul and repair facilities. Here the *Cardiff Queen* lies alongside with the fitters assembled on the after-end of the paddle-box where the small boat landing-steps can also been seen. The yard and its machinery are currently being restored as a tourist attraction. *Nick James*

THE CAMPBELL PURSERS: A SPECIAL BREED

The Campbell Pursers were a very special breed. Not only were they responsible for ticket sales and looking after the cash – that is where the public encountered them – but, after the introduction of ship-to-shore radio, the Purser also tended to double as Radio Operator.

The late Charles Wall joined Campbells after the Second World War. He was Marconi-trained (1928–9) and attached, as was the custom, to a British company, his being the Blue Funnel Line. His war experiences were grim; he was on Malta convoy duty and at the Sicily landings. His first sinking was in the Mediterranean, then his ship was mined during the Normandy landings. By an ironic twist of fate, the third ship to sink under him hit a mine in the Yangtze River late in 1946 – long after the war was over.

'He had had enough of the sea,' his wife, Fay, recalled ruefully. 'Never again!' However, Campbells persuaded him to join the *Glen Usk*, in 1947, transferring to the *Ravenswood* (Capt. Spong) and then the *Cardiff Queen* (Capt. Shedden). In 1948 it was was the *Britannia* (Capt. Phillips) and thence to the *Cardiff Queen* (Capt. J.A. Harris). Charles Wall also spent 1949 on the *Cardiff Queen*, seeing the season through. The *Glen Gower* was his home for 1950 and 1951 under Capt. Phillips. He continued with Campbells – a well known and respected figure – until the demise of the paddlers.

Fellow Pursers, Fay Wall remembered, were Jim Keating, Bill Berry and John Whiting. Such key personnel were often kept on during the winter; 'It would be chipping and scraping then...!'

Fay's family roots were in Pill, the Somerset village on the banks of the Avon, famous for its tradition of pilots and seafarers, and the Stenner family contributed much to the River and beyond. Her father, Frank Stenner, handled a pilot boat skiff at the age of ten and later joined Campbells after the First World War on the *Westward Ho*, while her mother, Nora, was a stewardess on the *Brighton Belle*.

Homecoming at the end of the season, when the paddlers came back from the South Coast, held especially vivid memories for the young Fay. The sun would be setting, its glow reflecting on the great, white bulk of the Spillers' mill at Avonmouth as the sound of paddles entered the river. 'We would go down to the river at Pill and wait for Mother, coming home. The *Brighton Belle* entered the Avon and came up the river, by Spillers, like a swan ... it was wonderful...'

Campbell's produced a delightful period timetable for May and June 1955 in the upper Channel. The twenties-style art-work seems to depict the *Glen Usk* and six-day season tickets for any sailings cost 35 shillings. (£1.75.)

TENBY HARBOUR AND BAY
WITH CAMPBELL STEAMER.

The two big post-war paddle steamers, the *Bristol Queen* and the *Cardiff Queen*, were able to offer a number of interesting long-distance excursions. Occasional visits to Milford Haven and Tenby were eagerly patronised by the enthusiasts as on this trip to Tenby in the mid-fifties by the *Cardiff Queen*.

It is interesting that Campbells, in addition to their regular services, increasingly time-tabled special visits and charter-trips, open to the public, in order to widen their cruising horizons. The later motor-ships continued to develop this facility. The concept of taking passengers to a place which they particularly wished to visit, at a time when a charter party particularly wanted to go there, sometimes in the evening after-work, inaugurated a subtle change of emphasis; the operator was able to rely financially on the charter fee (whatever the weather) while the passenger was required to make a stronger commitment to travel. This formula has become an essential, current part of the Waverley organisation's survival plan for steamer operations.

BIDEFORD, N'DEVON./64.

The trip up the River Torridge to Bideford Quay made a delightful excursion. The two Queens – here it is *Bristol Queen* – made regular visits, usually from Ilfracombe with a coach return for Bideford passengers. The shallowness of the estuary meant the steamer must arrive at high water, having embarked a pilot at Appledore Bar.

HAND ON THE GOLDEN LEVERS

The last two years of the *Glen Usk*'s active career were 1959 and 1960. Her second engineer, Roy Barclay, developed quite an affection for her; 'It was a smashing little engine-room. She had brass splash trays and open sky-lights; when the sun came down at mid-day it could almost blind you. A smart job!'

A decision to retire the *Glen Usk* had evidently been taken quite early in the 1960 season. Her bunkers were capable of accommodating 42 tons of lump coal but she appeared to get slower as the season progressed. Her normal pressure was 120 psi. though sometimes the engineers were lucky to get 80; it transpired that when she was coaled the request to remove the slack at the back of the bunkers was ignored. When the *Glen Usk* tied up in Penarth Dock for the last time there were 20 tons of black dust at the back of the bunkers and her boiler, George Owen recalls, was badly clogged with mud. A sad little postscript.

The engine-room team of the *Bristol Queen*, 1964-65; left to right Roy Barclay (2nd. Engineer), Reg Nieth (Chief Engineer), David Webb (3rd. Engineer).

Roy Barclay

Roy Barclay saw service on both the *Cardiff Queen* and *Bristol Queen* between 1961 and 1966 but he took a particular pride in the latter ship for a special reason. Roy was apprenticed pre-war to Charles Hill & Son, the Bristol ship-builders and, having served in tankers on Russian convoy duty, returned to Hills in 1946 as a marine fitter.

The company was hard at work on a new paddle steamer for P. & A. Campbell – the *Bristol Queen*. 'I helped to build her and I worked on her while the engines from

Rankin & Blackmore, Greenock, were being fitted. She was a lovely ship...' After ten years with Hills, Roy joined Campbells as an engineer; '...and there I was, at the 'golden levers', on the *Bristol Queen*, a ship I'd built. I was proud of that. It must be something of a record!'

The life of a sea-going engineer on the two Queens was an arduous one and the hours were long. In the later years, when money was short for proper winter overhauls, there were many small jobs to be done at night after the last passengers had gone ashore.

Re-fuelling usually took place on Thursday night when sleep was at a premium; the road tanker arrived at 1.00 a.m. and it would be 2.30 before the duty engineer saw his bunk, then it was up at 6 o'clock to raise steam for the next day's sailing. Principal bunker points were Swansea (Pockett's Wharf), Bristol (Cumberland Basin), Barry Pontoon and occasionally Ilfracombe, when the tanker came up from Exeter. 'Some nights, we would go to anchor and the steam was shut off. The tide would send the wheels spinning,' an eerie sensation, at the dead of night, Roy recalled.

By contrast, on a busy day, the *Bristol Queen*'s engine-room alley-ways were full of life; there were the cold and the curious, the 'regulars', too, stopping by for a chat, to ask questions and to reminisce. The majestic set of triple expansion engines was a natural focus for passengers' attention. Happily, a similar set from the same makers is still in existence in the preserved paddle steamer *Waverley*.

SALUTE TO THE QUEENS
THE BRISTOL QUEEN

It is an author's privilege to be partial in his affection for particular steamers and, occasionally, even self-indulgent. At the risk of sparking deep and learned debate, I boldly nail my flag to the masthead of the *Bristol Queen* and say that I loved that ship beyond all others.

I made my first trip on a paddle-steamer in 1949; I was an impressionable eight-year-old and the *Bristol Queen*

took us from Clevedon to Lynmouth for the day. I was introduced to the strange ritual of deck-chairs, on the Reserved Deck, which conferred an unexpected status on one so young. It was only realised later that our guardian viewed one shilling and sixpence as a fair price to keep us out of harm's (and other people's) way.

The day was a succession of new thrills, beginning with

White funnels and upper-works show up beautifully against the background of the Avon Gorge. The *Bristol Queen* has just cast off from Hotwells Pontoon .The Gorge opens up towards the Sea Walls, towering above the Portway. The *Bristol Queen* shows off the graceful flare of her bow from this angle. (4 June 1949).

a picnic lunch on deck – mounds of Marmite sandwiches and a hard-boiled egg – followed by the motor-boat trip from ship to shore at Lynmouth, a stomach-churning adventure in winds which may well have been of hurricane force. Certainly, there was enough salt on my face to steer my subsequent reading towards the Hornblower novels.

High tea was the climax of the homeward trip; the dramatic significance of eating in a Dining Saloon was only equalled by the menu. Not just that fish and chips were usually forbidden fare at home, but only grown-ups ever visited saloons, and this one even had waiters. I was close to heaven.

To be honest, I remember little about the engines, that day. The *Bristol Queen*'s engines were awesomely big and the glinting steel leapt in directions which seemed quite unreasonable and only just under control. It would have helped had I been taller... but the sound they made... the steady, unfaltering rhythm... the sound was unforgettable. I was captivated.

The view from *Bristol Queen*'s bridge as she passes Bridge Valley Road. Capt. Jack George in command with probably, Capt. John Wide as Mate at the wheel. (1960s).

The *Bristol Queen* rounds the Horseshoe Bend in the River Avon. (1960s). *Capt. Peter Tambling*

Some four years later, an enlightened school-master introduced me to the majestic, controlled brilliance of John Milton's poetry and by the time I came to study for exams, those early sounds in the engine-room of the *Bristol Queen* told me what my ears had been hearing. Here was the mechanical poetry of great engines, not the tripping metre of lightweight verse but music of epic stature, condensed, controlled and economic. The machinery composed its own stately grandeur in its movement, rising and falling with plunging cadences, accompanied by the rich vocabulary of hissing pistons and gliding, shining plates. It was a feast for the senses to feed upon.

All paddle-steamers give me pleasure but the *Bristol Queen* holds a very special place in my imagination. My sadness at her end was deep and strangely personal. Paradise Lost, indeed.

My tribute to the *Bristol Queen* is an imaginary trip down-Channel, from Bristol, using photographs shot on several different occasions during her short career. Such a thematic treatment might upset the chronology of the purist

Two deck views of the *Bristol Queen* illustrate the generous proportions of her promenade space. The rake of mast and funnels add a pleasing sense of urgency, while the solid, wooden handrail and the thick belting surrounding the paddle-box give a feeling of robustness, which particularly characterised this fine steamer. The deck-chairs are a curiosity; a number were acquired when the *St Trillo* joined the Campbell fleet in 1963 and you can see, on the seats, the woven Prince of Wales feathers and burgee of the defunct Liverpool & North Wales Steamship Co. Ltd. The photos were taken on 23 July 1967. Sadly it was destined to be my very last excursion on a White Funnel paddle steamer; little more than a month later the *Bristol Quee*n was withdrawn from service.

but it is through impressions of this beautiful paddle steamer in particular places that I am most stirred.

First sighting of the day could be contrived in two ways. I might leave the early bus at the top entrance of Ashton Court and pay my 1d toll to cross the Suspension Bridge; then it was down to the Hotwells Pontoon by the zig-zag path with its surprising glimpses. If I alighted at Cumberland Basin, the broadside view from Rownham Hill was worth the risk of the swing-bridge being closed for a shipping movement (though hot-footing it over the lock-gates offered an emergency route).

Once on board, I was able to make the transition – as I still do today on the *Waverley* or the *Balmoral* – from voyeur to voyager. I much enjoy the sash windows going up along St Vincent's Parade, above the busy Portway; the Avon leg of the trip is for waving. It's an idiosyncratic hobby, but I enjoy it unashamedly. Shore folk like to see the ships pass, so I wave...at Sea Mills, on the Horseshoe

Bend, at Pill and, a few minutes later, at Battery Point especially when the family come down to see us pass.

We don't call at Portishead so often, now; it was a regular late call on Sunday evenings, unless the steamer beat the Albright boat to the dock entrance. If the *Bristol Queen* hadn't met the morning's sand boats in Sea Mills Reach, coming up on the tide with their golden cargo from the Holms, she invariably passed them – the *Camerton* or the *Steep Holm*, perhaps – somewhere in Walton Bay when they were outward bound.

On the way down, Clevedon came next. By tradition there would always be a sonorous blast from the *Bristol Queen*'s whistle as we passed the bungalows above Ladye Bay when a white sheet would be held out and waved in greeting. The Managing Director, Clifton Smith-Cox, lived further up behind in Edgehill Road and he would be reassured that all was well.

The Clevedon call was always supervised by Bernard

Faraway, the Piermaster, whose allegiance to the U.D.C. and Campbells was finely balanced, though the former actually owned the pier. Latecomers were often a problem, so Mrs. Faraway raised a flag on an improvised flag-pole at the turnstile to let her husband know that the last of the passengers were on their way. Later a telephone was installed.

Crossing the Channel to Cardiff in the early sixties was always interesting and most of the shipping was British – the dramatic decline of our merchant fleet was yet to come. Half-way over, the *Bristol Queen* passed the English & Welsh Grounds lightship, our cheerful greetings enlivening the keepers' lonely existence.

At Cardiff pontoon the paddler's stern rope was sculled ashore to a pier-head bollard to help pull the bows round; when we sailed the dripping rope went so taut with the effort that you could have played a tune on it before it was released with a resounding splash, to be coiled aboard as

we went ahead. Penarth Pier followed and, then, it was round Lavernock Point to Barry, our final pick-up point on the Welsh side. Here we shared the pontoon with the pilot cutters which busily stepped aside to let us berth.

The departure from Barry was always an occasion to be up on deck; nowhere else in the whole channel did the *Bristol Queen* sound her siren so beautifully. The first three blasts for going

The *Bristol Queen* arriving at Penarth.
Trevor Morgan

The *Bristol Queen* has made her Penarth call and heads into a stiff, autumnal breeze. Capt. Jack George is on the bridge. (22 September 1951).

astern were pulled at the pontoon just to say she was on her way and the stone wall, standing tall beside the ship, bounced the great echoes to and fro in the confined space until the whole of Barry knew that she was off. Then there were three further blasts of warning just inside the breakwater, another acoustic sound-box, as the capstans chattered, drawing in the mooring ropes, until the *Bristol Queen* was finally liberated into the Channel's open water. A unique recording was made of this and other sounds; I play it often and there is still the same thrill as I listen and remember.

A little over an hour later we picked up the towering North Devon coastline at Lynmouth's Foreland Point. Sometimes the lighthouse keepers set off the fog-horn in greeting and came out on the terrace high above, to wave to us. Round the corner in the sheltered bay there was simple enjoyment, watching passengers go ashore by small launch.

Another hour and we stepped ashore ourselves at Ilfracombe, content to walk, eat ice-creams, climb hills, go shopping or visit the museum, happy in the knowledge that we had the whole of the return trip to look forward to, especially the wonderful serenity of the River Avon at the end of the day.

Experience of that evening trip up to Bristol on the *Bristol Queen* was a magical conclusion as, first, we passed the bright lights of the Pill pubs and The Lamplighters on the other bank. A short distance above Pill the dense foliage of Hung Road almost seemed to envelop the steamer as she curved left-handed into the Horseshoe Bend, the steady beat of the paddles echoing hollowly against the rocky ledges.

If it had been a hot day, a thin mist would be starting to rise off the pasture below Abbots Leigh and warm farmyard smells wafted off the land and spilled over into the river.In Sea Mills Reach the paddle-beats quickened and you felt the steamer heave herself forward; there was a wave from the dimly lit window of the Signal Station to say that the river was clear.

Last lap...into the darkness of the Gorge...thumps of paddles and swash of our wake on either bank behind us.

Journey's end for most passengers and time ashore for the many delights of Ilfracombe. The rugged cliffs of Hillsborough are a grand backdrop as the *Bristol Queen* makes for the pier. (14 August 1948).
Bristol Museum

Soon, too soon, the clatter of engine-room bells rang below us, Hotwells pontoon slid alongside us and the *Bristol Queen* was home.

It will never be quite the same but the greatest marvel is that those treasured sights and sounds can still be enjoyed today on the *Waverley* and the *Balmoral*. The age-old magic, the same sense of occasion is still there.

Undergoing overhaul in Penarth Dock the *Bristol Queen* has been raised on the pontoon for inspection and painting. *Trevor Morgan*

CARDIFF QUEEN

I certainly do not wish to take anything away from the *Cardiff Queen*; this fine paddle steamer also had her devotees. Her life-span (1947-66) was even shorter than that of the *Bristol Queen*, her near-sister. She, too, was an exceptionally good-looking ship and graced the Bristol Channel on her long-distance excursions for all but two years of her career (1952-3), when she was away on the South Coast.

Though a mere four feet shorter, the *Cardiff Queen* (765 grt) had an altogether lighter feel about her in comparison with the *Bristol Queen* (961 grt). It wasn't just a matter of tonnage, which can hide technical differences in

Fresh from the Clyde on her delivery voyage, the *Cardiff Queen* enters Cumberland Basin, Bristol for the first time on 19 June 1947. The *Empress Queen*, whose stern is just visible, had arrived back from her post-war refit the previous evening.   *Bristol Museum*

The infamous Horseshoe Bend claims another victim; on 27 July 1947 the *Cardiff Queen* grounded briefly on a rising morning tide. The tug *John King* stood by but all was well.

Grahame Farr collection

Looking forward to Avonmouth on the starboard side; the *Cardiff Queen*'s funnels rise above the reserve deck aft. Underneath it there was a comfortable, small saloon bar. *Bristol Museum*

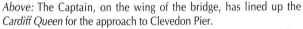

Above: The Captain, on the wing of the bridge, has lined up the *Cardiff Queen* for the approach to Clevedon Pier.

Capt. Peter Tambling

Above right: A good crowd awaits on the landing jetty as the *Cardiff Queen* arrives at Birnbeck Pier, Weston.   *Capt. Peter Tambling*

Right: A deck view on board the *Cardiff Queen.* The boxes for life-jackets, in the foreground, made for hard seating but were better than nothing on a busy day   *Capt. Peter Tambling*

measurement, but rather an impression. The *Bristol Queen,* for example, carried two extra lifeboats aft, on the promenade deck (which were, incidentally, soon raised to allow seated passengers a better view) and her bridge deck extended above the forward deck house.

An important differentiating feature was the attractive wooden surround on the *Cardiff Queen*'s bridge; many would say that this traditional touch enhanced the steamer's appearance. Both paddlers shared the same sense of dignity and speed but the *Cardiff Queen* was undoubtedly the demurer of the two; she was more the coquette than the solid matron.

Against the background of the work-shed between the first and second Mountstuart dry-docks at Cardiff, the *Cardiff Queen* waits to leave the pontoon. Only the gangway of the other embarkation point remains, hanging forlornly in mid-air. It was difficult for the steamers to gain clearance as they went astern towards the Bute Dock entrance, out of sight to the right of the picture. The skiff in the foreground will, shortly, collect a stern rope and row it back to a bollard in front of the Pier Head building to assist the speedy canting of the paddler. This picture was taken in 1964.

Courtesy Bernard Rackley

The fine lines of the *Cardiff Queen* are shown off to perfection in this photograph from 1951. The elegant flare of the bows – less pronounced than her sister – and the nicely raked funnels give her a most attractive appearance as she sets out from Swansea.

Bristol Museum

Capt. George Gunn on the bridge of the *Cardiff Queen* at Ilfracombe, during the 1956 season. On each wing, for berthing, stands an engine-room telegraph (on the outside) and a docking telegraph; the latter, connected to repeaters forward, aft and in the waist, advised the ropemen when to make fast, heave in, slack away or let go. The thin cord across the centre controlled the whistle and the voice-pipe to the engine-room can clearly be seen at the rear of the bridge. The *Bristol Queen* had the luxury of a telephone!

Bristol Museum

THE TWO QUEENS: FINALE.

Whenever you saw the *Bristol Queen* and the *Cardiff Queen*, the last flowering of the great Campbell paddle steamer inheritance, the two ships were a joy to watch.

They were so graceful in movement; even berthed at a pier they possessed an impressive dignity. From the moment the paddles began to turn it was exciting to anticipate their arrival and they were majestic in the brief moment of their passing. The feeling of wistfulness that you were not on board was matched by a sense of pride that

Final voyage on 9 April 1968; it was but a short tow from Newport Docks, up the River Usk to Cashmore's ship-breaking yard. John Critchley, owner of Weston's Birnbeck Pier, had made an unsuccessful attempt to moor the *Cardiff Queen* in the Usk, preparatory to turning her into a floating night-club. Had he succeeded, the growing zest for preservation might just have secured her future.   *Bristol Museum.*

you had watched them go by.

The departure of the two Queens from the Bristol Channel made it an emptier and a duller place.

Campbells' second motor-ship was the *Vecta*, built in 1938 for the Southampton – Isle of Wight service of Red Funnel Steamers. The *Vecta* made her debut at Ilfracombe on 27 September 1965 where she is seen arriving with a good gathering of 'regulars', augmented by the curious. The following year she adopted White Funnel colours and became the *Westward Ho*. Her service in the Bristol Channel ended in September 1971 and she subsequently became a Manchester 'flotaurant'. *Bristol Museum*

According to contemporary sources the little *St Trillo* had her following. P. & A. Campbell chartered her from Townsend Ferries who had acquired her from the Liverpool and North Wales Steamship Co. Ltd. She had started life as the *St Silio* (314 grt) in 1936 and her builders were Fairfield Ship Building & Engineering Co. who installed two 12 cylinder Crossley diesels. Renamed *St Trillo* after the war she finally found her way into the White Funnel Fleet for the 1963 to 1969 seasons. I certainly remember her as a comfortable ship, if rather slow, and much roomier than her appearance might indicate. This photograph was taken at Bristol on 13 April 1963 at the start of her first trip to Ilfracombe.

Bristol Museum

The *Devonia* and the *Balmoral* (outside) laying up at The Grove, Bristol on 26 October 1978 in their winter quarters.

Grahame Farr collection

On the same day that *Waverley* first arrived at Barry, 30 May 1979, the last of the White Funnel ships, the *Balmoral,* is pictured leaving Penarth. The *Balmoral* had one more Bristol Channel season in front of her before being put up for sale and disposal.

Ian Shannon collection

PART FOUR
THE WAVERLEY YEARS:
MAINTAINING THE GREAT TRADITION

In 1979, while on a positioning voyage from Glasgow to the South Coast, the *Waverley* met bad weather at the mouth of the Bristol Channel. This picture of her, sheltering on 12 April in St Ives harbour, must record one of the *Waverley*'s most unusual calls. She is battened down for the long trip with steel deadlights slotted over the saloon windows. One of the *Waverley* directors, Joe McKendrick, travelling with the ship, reported a brisk trade in souvenirs from the ship's shop at this unexpected venue!
S. Bennetts

To the casual observer this photograph might appear rather unremarkable; a dock entrance and its cluster of squat offices. The two-funnelled ship has arrived in the rain, witness the umbrellas of the onlookers, but the lines of bunting suggest a special occasion. In fact, it marked an arrival which many people had treasured in their dreams but had almost put beyond the bounds of possibility; after twelve long years a paddle steamer was in service again on the Bristol Channel.

The *Waverley*'s arrival at Barry on 30 May 1979 for a long week-end of sailings was an emotional rekindling of the past glories of paddle power.

The atmosphere of that first long week-end in the Bristol Channel was incredible; wherever the *Waverley* called, there was an air of excitement fuelled by strong media coverage.Long queues of passengers evoked memories of earlier days and gave the all important pointer to a strong and affectionate interest which could be built on for future seasons. Some of these historic moments were recorded by the camera of the late Ian Shannon.

Ian Shannon collection

The *Waverley*'s first arrival at Penarth on 31 May 1979. A classic view, with Brean Down looming out of the haze, Flat Holm and its white pencil of a lighthouse, Steep Holm on the right.

Ian Shannon collection

First call at Avonmouth 1 June 1979. Not an easy pier, as passengers have to be bussed through the docks.   *Ian Shannon collection*

PRINCE IVANHOE

The arrival of the *Prince Ivanhoe* in the Bristol Channel in May 1981 was a development which local cruising enthusiasts found as exciting as it was unexpected.

Friends of the Waverley organisation had bought the *Prince Ivanhoe* as a running-mate for the paddle steamer *Waverley*; it was felt that the former Isle of Wight motor ship – *Shanklin* was her previous name – offered greater security for the vintage paddler, especially if there were recurrent boiler problems.

There was an added incentive for the purchase of this well appointed excursion ship; a Clyde cruising subsidy had been paid to Caledonian MacBrayne in 1980 for what was generally felt to be a less attractive programme than

The *Prince Ivanhoe* is pictured alongside the Arnolfini Centre in Bristol City Docks on 4 May 1981, on her very first visit. She was owned by the Firth of Clyde Steam Packet Co., having originally been completed in 1951 by Denny Bros., Dumbarton, for the Portsmouth to Ryde railway service. With a gross tonnage of 986 she was exceeded in size (on Bristol Channel excursions) only by Campbell's *Empress Queen* . *Ian Shannon collection*

the one the Waverley organisation could offer with two genuine cruise ships.

Much to the Waverley organisation's chagrin the whole subsidy for 1981, £100,000, went to the Loch Lomond steamer, the *Maid of Loch*. There was certainly no future for the *Prince Ivanhoe* on the Clyde without a subsidy.

Fortuitously, there was an opening. The last throw of White Funnel Steamers Ltd., the joint Campbell-Landmark Trust venture of 1980, had been more costly than the Trust had reckoned. When the agreement terminated at the end of that season, the *Balmoral*, like the languishing *Devonia*, was also put up for sale.

One door had closed for the *Prince Ivanhoe* – the Clyde. Following the withdrawal of the *Balmoral*, another door was excitingly opened. For the P*rince Ivanhoe* the Bristol Channel beckoned.

Following repairs to the port main engine, interior reconstruction work and numerous other tasks to fit the

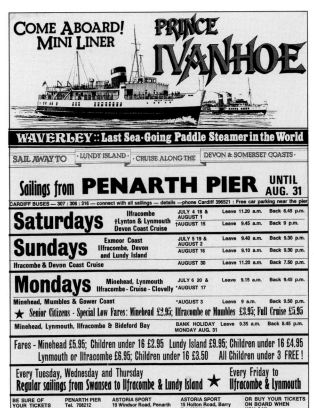

Viewed on 5 May, the *Prince Ivanhoe* passes Leigh Woods on her outward trip to Barry for repairs.   *Ian Shannon collection*

Prince Ivanhoe for her new role – the facilities at the Waverley terminal in Glasgow proving invaluable – the motor-ship finally made ready for sea with a visit to Govan dry-dock. Although she had arrived in the Clyde the previous November, it was the hectic two month's work in March and April 1981 which enabled the *Prince Ivanhoe* to make her début at Bristol on 1 May, for inspection by the public.

Unfortunately she had sustained bottom damage on some rocks on the Leigh Woods side on her way up-river

The *Prince Ivanhoe* leaves Penarth on a cruise on 28 June 1981. Her spacious, open decks were an outstanding feature for passengers to enjoy the passing scenery.
Alan Kittridge

and had to visit the dry-dock at Barry four days later. Despite this setback the *Prince Ivanhoe* drew very favourable comment from public and enthusiasts alike and she settled down to an increasingly successful patronage as the summer progressed.

There were short spells of Clyde service, the longest when she acted for the *Waverley* during the latter's Bristol Channel visit. The *Prince Ivanhoe*'s main Bristol Channel season began on 23 June.

It had been an uplifting, if somewhat anxious experience to ensure that this new venture was a success. As Chairman of the local branch of the Paddle Steamer

Preservation Society, I had arranged meetings with tourist and local authority leisure interests who accepted the new principle that the *Prince Ivanhoe* could run only with their help, a measure of finance and lots of publicity. It is a formula on which the *Balmoral* still relies.

Although the ship was crewed professionally, there was a willing pool of part-time stewards, pursers, rope-handlers, shop-keepers and publicity distributors from within the ranks of the Society. I was not alone in rolling up my sleeves and cleaning out the lavatories, sweeping lounges and washing glasses in the bar; we were all deeply committed to our new charge. If cruising in the Bristol Channel was to continue – and we desperately desired it – that's how it had to be.

Good weather and, it seemed, word of mouth were at last lengthening the passenger queues and by the beginning of August it was clear that the *Prince Ivanhoe*

had won acceptance.

The dream was cruelly and devastatingly shattered on the afternoon of the 3 August. During a Gower Coast cruise the *Prince Ivanhoe* was holed off Port Eynon Point and beached at Horton, her final resting place. Opinions differed, but whether it was rocks or an uncharted wreck which had inflicted the damage, the wound was mortal.

My intense relief that all 450 passengers were evacuated safely was matched with a deep desolation. That I had watched and photographed the *Prince Ivanhoe*, sailing purposefully down the Avon, only the day before, heightened my sense of anguish.

Apart from the rescue operation, the only redeeming feature of the incident was that the highly capable and committed company personnel were absolved from blame at the subsequent inquiry into the ship's loss. The events are covered in Alan Brown's excellent book *Shanklin: Ill Fated Prince*.

Once again it looked as though the Bristol Channel would be without a full-time excursion ship.

Port Eynon Bay, 3 August 1981.
South Wales Evening Post

BALMORAL REBORN

The closure of P. & A. Campbell's Bristol Channel services in 1980 and the subsequent sale of the *Balmoral*, to become a floating restaurant in Dundee, seemed to spell the end of active life for this sturdy and popular motor-ship.

Despite the profound disappointment of the *Prince Ivanhoe* venture in 1981 the Waverley organisation determined to persist in its objective of acquiring a second ship.

There was much rejoicing when *Balmoral* was selected, after rigorous examination, to become the *Waverley*'s running-mate. No-one in the Bristol Channel had seriously expected to see her again. Some sceptics felt that her condition would make her too costly to renovate, but much replating was achieved and many improvements made to her interior.

Some purists regarded the *Balmoral* as an interloper in a steamer-orientated outfit but there were good reasons for choosing her. A shallow draught makes her *Waverley*'s equal but her slender beam allows her to visit destinations which the paddler could not attempt. Like the *Waverley*, engine spares often have to be individually cast and the problem of both quality and availability is a melancholy paradigm of the collapse of Britain's maritime status.

More compelling reasons, however, lay behind the acquisition of the *Balmoral*. The Bristol Channel is essential to the *Waverley*'s financial health; her operation in traditional paddle steamer waters has built up an enthusiastic and valuable following. The *Balmoral*'s summer services, here, ably complement and build on that popularity and she, too, is a vintage ship in her own right.

Fund-raising on board is an ongoing and essential Society commitment, while the shops are run entirely by volunteers. The sale of souvenirs, books and confectionery

There is only one worse place than a dry-dock and that is the 'knacker's yard'. No seaman enjoys this important annual occasion when a ship is lifeless, dead, quite out of her element. The *Balmoral* was overhauled in Bristol during the winter of 1988 and dry-docked next to the *Great Britain* in April 1989. High and dry, the *Balmoral* accepts an opportunity for underwater replating and high-pressure hosing (below, left) ready for the hull to be painted for the season ahead. Suitable dry-docks are not so easy to find and this local facility is greatly appreciated.

Bristol United Press

is an area which has been very successfully developed. Curiously, Campbells never paid much attention to it. Today's approach is a far cry from the chocolate boys of yore!

There is no shadow of a doubt that the Waverley organisation's concern for the Bristol Channel, with the support of the Paddle Steamer Preservation Society, has safeguarded the future of big-ship excursions. The ultimate arbiter, however, is public patronage.

The very first ship to call at the restored Clevedon Pier was the *Balmoral* on 9 May 1989. It was adjudged a sensible precaution for the *Balmoral* to do berthing trials – which were completely successful – before the official opening. Capt. Stephen Michel is easing the *Balmoral* alongside the landing-stage which, although the most exposed part of the structure, required the least remedial attention at the time. The *Balmoral*'s Mate, Ted Davies, is keeping a look-out on the wing of the bridge.

Clevedon Printing Co.

The ongoing restoration and maintenance of the *Balmoral*'s twin Sirron diesels is in the experienced hands of her Chief Engineer, Ian McMillan (right). Relief Chief, Ian Muir (left) had served on both the *Waverley* and the *Balmoral* when this picture was taken, in 1988. New parts for the machinery of both ships frequently have to be forged to unique specifications. The preservation movement is therefore indebted to engineers like these. Their skill in seeking out scrap installations, adapting old spare parts, refining the operation of engines and all- important auxiliaries, calling up expertise from outside sources to do unusual tasks and giving the ships a trouble-free season on demanding schedules calls for the highest dedication. Overseer in this department for several seasons, Ian McMillan is a key figure in the continuing success of the *Waverley* and the *Balmoral*.   *Alan Brown*

THE RIVER WYE EXCURSION

The Wye Valley is very beautiful, particularly the stretch which snakes up past the beetling climber's crag of Symonds Yat. Campbells used to visit the river up to 1914, but only as far as Chepstow, the excursion ships then, as now, being limited by the road and rail bridges.

The *St Trillo* made some trips in the 1960s calling at the Buffer Wharf, Chepstow. One Saturday afternoon, 1 May

First picture in a sequence taken on 30 August, 1990, outlines the *Balmoral* against the trees as she comes up the River Wye.

Richard Clammer

1965, I remember using the *St Trillo* as a 'ferry' from my home in Portishead to Chepstow, then on to my work in Gloucester by train; The Purser was kind enough to treat my request for a 'single to Chepstow' generously. Perhaps it was my suitcase which softened his heart; summer passengers with luggage and camera always went on holiday down-Channel. He gave me – the only one ashore – a look of departing pity as I threaded my way between the heaps of sand on the wharf.

To-day, it is the *Balmoral* which makes the highly

The tight turn at Chepstow bridge requires slack water on the top of the tide. It has become a tradition to reward the Captain with a generous round of applause for his skill and judgement.

Richard Clammer

popular excursions up the River Wye. There are usually two each season, starting from Penarth and calling at Clevedon, where a Pilot comes aboard to renew acquaintance with this rare destination.

The low-slung road bridge bearing the M4 into the Principality is the first obstacle. Entering the Wye on the top of a neap tide, the *Balmoral* has just enough mast clearance with adequate water beneath her. The river winds its way past the former Beachley Army Apprentices College to starboard while thick woodland mounts up on the other side. Then, to port, the slipways of the old shipyard come into view. Big ships were built here in a hurry during the First World War on adjacent stocks; when the first Severn motorway bridge was built, sections constructed in the yard were floated on barges down to the site.

At last, confronted by the new Chepstow road bridge, the *Balmoral* can go no further. In the rocky pool below Tutshill, one engine going full astern and the other full ahead, the *Balmoral* performs a graceful and dramatic pirouette to face downstream and so to the sea.

The spectacle is not over yet. Helm to port at the mouth of the Wye, the *Balmoral* rejoins the Severn's stream to make her awe-inspiring run between the twin towers of one of the world's great suspension bridges.

The camera of Richard Clammer has magnificently caught the atmosphere of this unique trip – its serenity, the controlled drama of the turn, the majesty of man's constructive genius as a climax.

The *Balmoral* passes beneath the first Severn road bridge; on an oblique approach, which keeps the ship in the deep-water channel.
Richard Clammer

It has always been part of the Waverley organisation's policy to explore some of the smaller Bristol Channel ports. There was much excitement at the Gloucestershire town of Lydney, a former Forest of Dean coal dock, when the *Balmoral* called there on 6 September 1991.

The *Balmoral* was on an afternoon excursion from Penarth and Clevedon. As the intricate warping can only be attempted at high water the Lydney passengers were returned by bus from Penarth later in the evening. A local photographer caught these wonderfully animated scenes at the Lydney lock entrance. It was a great family occasion.

Steve Cassidy

It is good to see an old Bristol Channel tradition kept up: a crew photograph at the end of the 1992 season, taken in October at the *Balmoral*'s winter lay-up berth, Prince's Wharf, Bristol. Back row (l. to r.): Scott Adam (Purser), Alec Scott (Bo'sun), Nick Worthy (Deck), Wilson McDougall (Relief Chief Eng.), Ian McMillan (Chief Eng.), Capt. Kit Lee (Relief Master), Lionel Vaughan (Shopkeeper), Oliver Scott (Motorman), Andy Gregory (Chief Steward), Graham Gellatly (First Officer), Capt. David Neill (Master). Front row (l. to r.): Barnaby Taraniuk, Stevie Williams, John O'Shea, Colin Hawthorne, Alec Wilson (Catering). If only past generations had put names to all their groups...!

Robert Coles

Newport calls for *Waverley* initially involved the use of the Queen Alexandra lock itself for movement of passengers. Although it was a cumbersome arrangement, sometimes having to lower and raise levels, the solid support from Newport made the effort most worthwhile. When the *Waverley* (693 grt) was built in 1947 by A. & J. Inglis, Glasgow, for simple Clyde ferry and excursion work, neither her builders nor those who travelled on her could possibly have envisaged the multitude of unusual visits, like this one, that she would later make, so far from home!   *Alan Kittridge*

Sharpness was used as a steamer call by Campbells a hundred years ago, with Midland train connections. Latterly the *Balmoral* made infrequent visits during her White Funnel days.

It fell to the historic paddle steamer *Waverley* to reopen the station for an early season call to convey passengers to Ilfracombe. This popular and unusual trip is a regular feature each summer and here on 9 June, 1990 the passengers from Cheltenham, Gloucester, Stroud and Berkeley Vale queue to board their own special excursion. Normally the Sharpness North Pier has been used but lack of barriers meant *Waverley* berthing at the original Old Dock entrance, right on high water. On *Waverley*'s bridge, left to right, George Beveridge (Chief Engineer), George Woollard (Pilot) and Capt. David Neill (Master) watch the embarkation.   *Lesley Davies*

The *Waverley* makes her first, historic approach to Knightstone. Familiar features are the elegant pavilion on the left and the causeway on the right; do you remember being 'last over' without getting your feet wet? And do you remember the panting engine, with a funnel like an old Union Pacific locomotive, which hauled the Marine Lake dredge on steel hawsers? The concrete engine-house is still there...   *Weston Mercury*

Safely moored, the *Waverley* visits Weston for the first time on 26 May, 1993. Thanks to Knightstone Leisure and Woodspring District Council, thick timber baulks on the facing wall and mooring posts were installed.

If you are lucky enough to return at dusk, Weston from the sea is a spectacular kaleidoscope of twinkling lights, the whole sweep of the Bay lit up from end to end. Tuly a wonderful experience.   *Weston Mercury*

The return of the steamers to Weston in 1993 was an occasion for much local rejoicing. The Old Pier at Birnbeck, much to the dismay of pier connoisseurs, has suffered a steady deterioration and has not been used since Campbell's *Balmoral* called there in 1979. Such scant respect for Eugenius Birch's slender masterpiece is most regrettable.

Occasional landings by the Waverley organisation at Anchor Head had been attempted but transfer by small boat is a time-consuming process. Therefore it came as a pleasant surprise to learn that the outside wall of Knightstone Island had been carefully surveyed and found suitable for steamer calls.

The *Waverley*'s first call on 26 May, 1993, evoked considerable interest and satisfaction that Weston, with its long tradition, was once again on the cruising timetable. Both the *Waverley* and the *Balmoral* made several calls during that season and again in following years. The imaginative management of the Waverley Steam Navigation Co. has

certainly made a virtue of necessity: not only was there no other possible landing-place, but Knightstone is also right at the very heart of the resort.

THE LUNDY CHURCH SERVICE

The evolution of Bristol Channel excursions, during the *Waverley* years, has moved away from the Campbell concept of regular services to the resorts. Although this element is the mainstay of operations, the *Waverley* and the *Balmoral* make much use of all-day charters, evening charity functions, school cruises, nominated sailings for P.S.P.S. members and cruises with a specific focus.

One such special occasion – when the weather allows – is the annual church service on Lundy Island. The dogged spirit of faith in the future and a remarkably ecumenical bond of friendship are two of the many qualities which help to bind the Paddle Steamer Preservation Society's membership together and they find their expression in sung evensong, once a year, in the granite, island church of St Helena.

The congregation at evensong. Other groups meet less formally at the Marisco Tavern or buy souvenirs at the Island Stores. It is important that visitors support the island's fragile economy. In this respect the Society's ships are great contributors to the places they visit.

Robert Coles

The *Waverley* visits Lundy for the annual church service on 17 June, 1984. Left to right are Neil McLeod (Second Officer, *P.S. Waverley*), the Rev. Colin Harrison (Catering Officer) who took the service, Nigel Coombes (Chairman of P.S.P.S. at the time).

Robert Coles

Passengers wait on the landing beach at Lundy to be ferried by the launch *Westward Ho* back to the steamer. In a most unusual manoeuvre the *Waverley* is moored to a large rock (out of sight on the right of the picture). The rope, visible well above the line of waiting passengers, helps to keep the bow pointing out ready for a quick departure to keep the arrival time at Portishead, in the evening.

Robert Coles

In its wider context it is undoubtedly true to say that without the Paddle Steamer Preservation Society there would be no excursion ships on the Bristol Channel or, indeed, anywhere else around our coastline. A combination of diverse skills is given freely, often without charge; craftsmen, carpenters, welders, painters, fitters, engineers and draughtsmen give up their time to help prepare the ships for each season. Retained professionals, officers and crews, make the *Waverley* and the *Balmoral* ready for sea and run them with skill and devotion during the long summer programmes.

Professional management staffs offices in Glasgow and Barry – the latter being responsible for Bristol Channel sailings – while the Society's third ship, the Edwardian river paddle steamer *Kingswear Castle*, runs and is administered from Chatham.

Capt. Neill and Mike Hogarth, Purser, help passengers to re-embark.
Robert Coles

At about midnight, a tired but happy ship's complement disembarks at Portishead. *Robert Coles*

My passion for passing on a living legacy of steamer excursions in the Bristol Channel lies in the belief that tradition is important. I am proud that the name of the historic port of Bristol should be displayed confidently under *Balmoral*'s name at the stern and on her life-belts.

When the *Waverley* paddles south from the Clyde each year, I think of the little White Funnel steamer *Waverley* which set out, over a hundred years ago, from the same Scottish river to establish a new and enduring tradition in southern waters.

In recent years official regulations for all passenger ships have meant the spending of large sums of money on improvements to the *Waverley* and the *Balmoral*. The raising of £350,000 by the start of the 1995 season – exclusive of revenue and from within the Paddle Steamer Preservation Society – was a great test of resolve and commitment.

The *Waverley*, the last of the great sea-going paddle steamers, and the *Balmoral*, the last member of the great White Funnel Fleet, are all that we have left. They add a dash of colour around our coasts and remind us of our heritage. I think that is something worth passing on.

119

ACKNOWLEDGEMENTS

I freely acknowledge my great debt to George Owen, the Bristol Channel steamer historian. As the elder statesman of all matters connected with the White Funnel fleet, George's advice has been significant: his recall of past Channel events and personalities is truly remarkable.

Many people have helped in the compilation of this book by lending photographs, offering information and generously giving up their time to talk to me. It has been a most happy and rewarding experience and I record their assistance with thanks:

Dr. Donald Anderson, Jim Ashford, Roy Barclay, S. Bennetts, The Rev. Norman Bird, Alan Brown, Lin Bryant, Steve Cassidy, Richard Clammer, Robert Coles, Ken Crowhurst, Lesley Davies, Austin Davis, Michael Farr (for access to the collection of his father, the late Grahame Farr), Jim Fraser, Syd Gray, Geofrey Hamer, Nick James, Ken Jenkins, Alan Kittridge, Mrs Anne Longley (Roedean School), Trevor Morgan, Flt. Lieut. John Oldham, Mrs Dorothy Partington, Eric Payne, Geoffrey Pritchard, Bernard Rackley, Sid Robinson, Mrs J. Slocombe (Ilfracombe Museum), Peter Southcombe, Terry Sylvester (Waverley Excursions Ltd.), Capt. Peter Tambling, Mike Tedstone, Keith Thomas, Philip Tolley, Mrs Elsie Tyrrell, Lionel Vaughan, Mrs Fay Wall, Paul Webb, Eddie Wood.

I am also very grateful to the following organisations:
The Bristol United Press,
Clevedon Printing Co.,
The Weston Mercury,
The Scottish Record Office,
Bristol Museum.

I attach the greatest importance to the work of press staff photographers.

Whilst I have credited all known sources, I apologise for any omissions.

My nephew, Edward Raymond, interrupted a busy life to type my manuscript: his perseverance and skill – in alien territory – was exemplary.

This is my second book from Twelveheads Press: may I again thank my publishers for their marvellous co-operation and encouragement at all stages. In particular, I could not have done without the sensitive guidance of Alan Kittridge: I am warmly appreciative of his artistic skill in matters of presentation, balance and overall design.

CAMPBELL'S

1937

TRIPS from

(Weather and circumstances permitting)

By Saloon Steamers " BRIGHTON QU

For Rail and Road Fa

 Out by AIR—Back by STEAMER or vice
Fare 14/-   (Intending passenger

Saturday, Aug. 14	Morning **CHANNEL CRUISE.**	Leave Palace Pier 11.0 a.m
	VENTNOR (Cheap Trip—1¼ hours ashore).	Leave Pa
	WORTHING (Single or Return by Rail or Road).	Leave Pa
	Afternoon **CRUISE off LITTLEHAMPTON**	Leave Palace
	Evening **CRUISE to SEVEN SISTERS**	Leave West Pier
Sunday, Aug. 15	Morning **CHANNEL CRUISE**	Leave Palace Pier 11.10 a.m.
	EASTBOURNE Leave West Pier 2.40 p.m. ;	Palace Pier
	EASTBOURNE (Cheap Trip—½ hour ashore)	Leave Wes